STOP MUCKING ABOUT & JUST WRITE YOUR BOOK

SARAH BULLEN & KATE EMMERSON
with Tessa Graham

First published in 2020 by
QuickShift Publishing
PO Box 698
Melville
Johannesburg
2109

ISBN: 978-0-620-85144-2 (print)

www.thewritingroom.co.za
www.kate-emmerson.com
www.tessagraham.com

Text by Kate Emmerson, Sarah Bullen and Tessa Graham
Copy edited by Lindsay Norman
Cover design by Callum Jagger
Typesetting by Book Lingo
Proofreading by Sean Fraser
Printed and bound by Print on Demand, Cape Town

Kate and Sarah run ridiculously good online mentorships for writers and have helped countless writers get their stories out into the world. We can push, prod and help you to 'WRITE YOUR BOOK in 100 DAY' to take you from Dream to Draft. The second level is a 10-week Bootcamp titled 'PITCH TO PUBLISHED'. Kate and Sarah also facilitate writing retreats and residencies in gorgeous, inspirational locations around the world.

DISCLAIMER

Sarah says, I have taught, written about and lectured in writing for so many years that I can't always remember what was my idea, and what I gleamed from some other writing coach. Much of this book has come from courses I have written, or Kate has written, over the past 10 years. If I have used any words or theories and claimed ownership in error, I apologize in advance as it was unintentional.

DEDICATION

It is just the best job in the world, working with stories, hearing tales from the heart and playing with words. So this book is firstly for all the magical stories that need to be told and the writers who bravely tell them.

Sarah – This book was a labour of love, but we also had so much fun writing it. It is for all my teachers along the way who have shown me the power of words, the power of discipline and the power of finishing what I start. It is also for all the writers I have worked with, laughed with, cried with and shared lives with. Finally, it is also for my children Ruby and Jude and my support team back home of Ingrid Roderick, John Roderick, Katherine Tullis and my mom—all of who—allow me to work ridiculous hours, travel and follow my passion.

Kate – This book is dedicated to YOU. Writing a book is one of life's most powerful journeys that you can ever embark on. It changed my life and I know it will do the same for you. You have been holding that spark of an idea close in your heart and daring to dream. Now it's time to listen to the whispers of your soul. You are brave. It's one hell of a ride becoming an author, so hold on tight and remember to have fun.

TABLE OF CONTENTS

'art One
'lan

TASK 1

What Have You Got Yourself Into?

> 'I took a deep breath and listened to the old brag of my heart
> I am, I am, I am.'
>
> **Sylvia Plath, The Bell Jar**

YOU HAVE IN YOUR HANDS a workbook that will support you as you write your very own book. Nervous? Excited? Hopefully a bit of both.

It often happens that when people start our mentorship they have an equal mixture of 'over-the-top' excitement and 'what-the-hell-have-I-done' nerves. And that is a great place to start.

You should feel excited and scared! You have made a massive commitment to Write Your Book in 100 Days and now you know that we very seldom let writers off the hook until they have finished their book.

You have paid good money to get us to boss you into it. Are you ready?

Perhaps you have decided to write your life story, or share something you have learned along the way. You may be very clear about the kind of book you want to write. On the other hand, you may have no cooking clue what you're going to write about, or what kind of story it will be.

But you have an urge, or a calling, to write it down. That's where we all start.

At the end of just over three months, you will have a book in your hand.

So how are you going to do this?

Here's how this book is going to work. It is practical and based on our years of walking writers down the path to publication.

There are a few parts to this that sort of add up to 100 days. Well, the working part does.

> **Part 1 [10 days] Plan. Time to design and plot your book**
>
> **Part 2 [90 days] Write! You write hard and fast with a view to getting down a minimum of 50,000 words**
>
> **Part 3 [30 days] Pause. Breathe. Put your first draft of your book aside and start to build your Author Brand**
>
> **Part 4 [30 days] You do your edit, second draft and proposal.**

For most of this workbook we are going to focus on the first 100 Days and we are going to push, prod and drive you to get to that point. What point? The point where you are sitting with your first draft in your hand.

The 100 Days deadline means you have 10 days of planning and 90 days of solid, frenzied writing to get you there. Easy? You bet.

As an added bonus, at the end of the process, we will walk you through the next steps you need to take to go all the way and publish your book—if that is what you want. We suggest that you dive in swiftly and complete Part 1 in about 10 days. Move fast. Then take about 90 days to work through Part 2 and complete your first draft. Then you can take a breather from your book while focusing on your author brand in Part 3. When you are ready to go all the way to publication, you move onto Part 4.

Perhaps until now you have written some blogs, an article, journaled, or a combination of them all. But now you are entering the realm of longer-form writing. This requires planning, as you will learn. It also requires diarizing writing time and blocking off entire days to write. Most of all, it requires tenacity and determination.

How are we going to help you?

Sarah says

The really exciting thing as an author is that there are SO MANY options and ways to get published in this day and age. Publishing a book is accessible, and a very legitimate way of getting your story out into the world. It's not as hard or as daunting as it was back when I sent off my first (regrettably very bad) book.

Back in 2002, book publishing was a totally different terrain. No publishers accepted emailed submissions. It had to be a printed hard copy and posted to them with an SASE (self-addressed stamped envelope). The first three chapters had to have 1.5 spacing with a 12-point font.

I headed to the Post Office with 10 thick envelopes, dug deep in my student wallet and sent them off to the top UK publishers via registered post. Then I waited. I got just one (posted) reply after six months, and it was not good news.

'Thank you for submitting your book. We will not be accepting it on our list. Good luck with your writing.' They used my SASE to return my work.

Like so many writers, I just gave up. It was partly embarrassment, but I'd also shelved that dream and moved on to something else during the long wait.

Fast-forward 17 years and writers are dealing with a totally different scenario. You can publish your own book. Publishers take submissions via online platforms such as submittable.com or via email, they are approachable and they don't really care what font size or spacing you use.

All publishers and agents are constantly on the lookout for some good, strong stories. Your job as a writer is to send them the best version of your book. We are going to get you there over the next few months.

A lot of this book process is very practical and simple. Some of it is hard and frustrating. But we promise you that if you follow the process and you do the work you will end up with a book.

You may want to write a book to change hearts and minds, or influence people and clients. You may want to gently record your life or honour someone else's.

Whatever you write, the process of writing remains the same. All writers need to walk the same path in order to get some form to their thoughts. Every writer needs to do The Work. There is not one writer who got published though talent alone. Talent has no real role in the hard work it takes to write a book. All of them got there through discipline, tenacity, and a lot of time on their bums with their fingers tapping on a keyboard.

Writing is not a social game. It is a solitary pursuit. You and your keyboard. I know how long and lonely it can be. I have written four book, I ghostwrite two a year, I have written about having cancer, having children, losing my husband, being in a coma and almost losing my own life. I have written about having to rebuild my body and life after an illness, and about surviving the things life throws in the way. Nothing will stop me sharing this stuff.

I believe that no matter what we go through, our ability to share our pain connects us as humans. Writing is such a lovely, clever and connecting way to share what you have learned.

Writing is a quiet place where you can construct words from letters, turn them into sentences, and tell your stories.

Books are longer, more carefully presented versions of your story. There are a lot more words to play with in a book and a lot more you can say. That is why you need to take care with them, and make sure that what you are writing has structure, pace and purpose.

My job as the writing coach is to structure your thoughts and ideas into a book. I don't like to settle for a book of random thoughts, I like your book to have structure and edge. I like books to get published and read.

Let's call me the architect.

⌘⌘⌘

Kate is the shifter, known as the Quick Shift Deva, and her role is to get you moving—fast! No messing about. Supporting, cajoling, and motivating, she will accept no excuses from you. Her role is to support you in bringing your best self to your best book. At times your writing journey will require you to dig deep, go within, face fears and limiting beliefs, shift perceptions and be willing to move forward when every part of you stubbornly refuses. Writing your book will absolutely demand that you call upon your inner strength, determination and tenacity.

She also knows what it takes to write a book—she has written and published four and is currently working on her fifth—*The Minimalist Manifesto*.

We both know how to help you construct your ideas into a workable format and find the inner determination to complete the task.

This workbook will get your book on the path to publication. Of course, not everyone wants to publish their books so you will also find there are some sections you can totally leave out.

At the end of every section or task throughout the book, you will find practical WRITING TASKS to complete. Make sure you do these before moving on to (or even reading) the next section. You will also find more soulful HEART EXERCISES to help you go deep within. Embrace them both to write your best book.

Here are some good reasons to write your story or write a book. How many are yours?

- ✓ To find meaning in your life
- ✓ You feel you have a powerful story to share
- ✓ You are an authority in your field
- ✓ You want to become an authority on a subject
- ✓ You want credibility
- ✓ To entertain people
- ✓ To leave a legacy
- ✓ You have no idea, just a calling
- ✓ You are not sure you even want to write a book
- ✓ You've been commissioned
- ✓ You have a good idea for a book
- ✓ You want to drive sales in your business
- ✓ You want to set the record straight
- ✓ You enjoy a challenge
- ✓ You find writing therapeutic
- ✓ You just feel the need to tell your story
- ✓ To make sense of the present by looking back at your past
- ✓ To re-witness the most important times in your life
- ✓ Explore guilt, fear, shame, anger
- ✓ To preserve your family's history
- ✓ To improve your ability to communicate with others
- ✓ To learn how to forgive yourself
- ✓ To confess something

- ✓ To record your life for your children
- ✓ You have a cause
- ✓ To write a speech for your political party
- ✓ To ensure that your children and grandchildren know who you are
- ✓ To inspire others to overcome difficulty
- ✓ To share a few tales your family love
- ✓ To share a wonderful life adventure
- ✓ To shine a light on a problem or cause
- ✓ To entertain readers with exciting/dramatic/amusing episodes from your life
- ✓ To teach an important lesson about your business, culture, religion, and so on
- ✓ To capture a slice of history
- ✓ To better understand yourself.

By the end of this book you will have

- ✓ Decided what format is best to share your story
- ✓ Found a working structure
- ✓ Found a story arc
- ✓ Teased out the Big Ideas you want to share
- ✓ Created your book outline
- ✓ Completed the first draft of your book.

WRITING TASK

Complete the statements below:

- My book is about …
- This story is important because …
- It interests ME because …
- It will show you (the reader) …
- I am qualified to tell it because …
- I think the key message of my book is …
- It will make you (the reader) …

think | laugh
| cry | rage | worry | relax |
be inspired | take more risks | change
| be better | see the light | understand |
want justice | join the movement | believe | bored
| change your thinking | angry | wonder | in awe |
irritated | question everything | feel hurt | confused |
happy | depressed | powerless | satisfied | connected
| smarter | wiser | introspective | humiliated | guilty |
inadequate | appreciative | respectful | peaceful | excited
| scared | delighted | motivated | disgusted | grateful |
lonely | fearful | vulnerable | exasperated |
humbled | challenged

Task 2
Should You Plan or Just Write?

> 'It makes more sense to write one big book—a novel or non-fiction narrative—than to write many stories or essays. Into a long, ambitious project you can fit or pour all you possess and learn.'
>
> **Annie Dillard**

I AM ASKED THIS ALL the time, Sarah says. Mostly by writers who are stuck four chapters into a book and they have told the whole story. The question always makes me smile (but inwardly I am doing a jaw-drop).

There is only one answer to this. Of course you should plan a book! You wouldn't build a bridge without a structural drawing, would you? You wouldn't take off on a hike through China without a map.

In fact, what often makes a book a 'good book', or a bestseller, is not the brilliance of the writing at all! It is the way the information is fed to the reader. It is the clarity of the concept, the argument and edge and the smart way in which the book is presented.

Planning a book is the writer's job. It is up to you to transform an idea into a solid, gripping and relatable book structure.

Planning a book requires a lot of focus. This is because a book is a long-form piece of writing. It is not an essay or a presentation. You will be asked to write a minimum of 50,000 words. That's a whole lot of writing!

What can make planning harder is that you have most of the information in your head already. Your head is packed with ideas, tips, stories, lessons, theories, jokes, memories or professional expertise. It's a lot of information to unpack and structure.

The processes in this workbook work on the TWO levels on which you need to tackle a book:

The first is the level of the heart

Most often this is your initial creative spark or idea. This is WHY you are here. You have been called to share your story, or any story.

This level comes with a crazy idea that grabs hold of a little piece of your heart. The idea goes like this … I want to write a book.

I want to write a book about …

- My sales expertise
- My battle with Crohn's disease
- Courage
- The power of love
- What it takes to slow down
- How to lose weight
- How to sell property
- How to raise stronger children
- How to make more money
- Making a container garden
- My walk through Tibet
- Addiction
- Forced removals
- My mad family

Sometimes you might be able to sit down and write a few pages and it flows like magic. But a full book is a longer endeavor.

Now that you've had your creative spark you need to turn it into a plot (or book outline).

The second level all books need is architectural or structural

This level is where you plan what your book is really about and how that is going to play out for the reader.

I believe in writing with a clear intention. This means you are writing with a clear end goal in mind. Most often the end goal is for your book to be published. Your end goal should most certainly be to end up with a book in your hand.

Once you have a clear idea of what your book is about, and you have selected a structure to support your book, your writing path becomes clear.

WRITING TASK

What is the golden thread that is going to hold your book together?

Take a look at the theme list in the Addendum and circle the themes that apply to your book. There should be a few. This is List 1: Themes that Bind your Book.

- Now focus on one word that sums up your book or your story.
- Get a sheet of paper (or use a page in your journal). In the center of the page write down one of the theme words from the theme list. Draw a circle around it.
- Create a mind map where you fill in the elements of your book that fit that theme.

Try to note down the following:

- What events, memories or moments from your life can you use to tell that story?
- What examples or anecdotes (not your own) should be used?
- What other stories or content may have a place in this book?
- How can it be organized in a logical way?
- What should not be in this book?

Start a new mind map using another theme word and see what patterns begin to emerge. Which events, anecdotes, memories or moments best tell your story?

HEART EXERCISE

Complete the sentences:

- The kind of books I LOVE to read are …
- These kinds of books leave me feeling …
- These kinds of books make me think about …
- If there is an emotion attached to these books it is …
- The tone/voice/vibe I like in an author is …

Task 3
Set Up Strong With Kate!

> 'What you think about, talk about, and get off your ass and do something about is what comes about!'
>
> **Larry Winget**

IN MY PROFESSIONAL LIFE, CULTIVATING a discipline of writing became the tool that took me the furthest. In fact, it took me, and my business, international. I am going to share my top 10 practical ways to make sure you set yourself up for writing success.

I always knew the power of writing down my thoughts. As a teenager, writing was my solace, a way to witness my own life. As I got older it became my internal dialogue, my therapy and a beautiful way of deepening my relationship with my world and myself, making sense of and expressing my emotions. I found a way to both record my life and process the stirrings in my heart along the way.

In 2003 I started a new career path when I qualified as an international Master Life Coach. At this time automation was the new buzzword in marketing, and writing a newsletter became a way of sharing my knowledge about this new trend called Life Coaching. It was also a way to share budding ideas and communicate with my clients. And, of course, reach new ones.

I started sharing my newsletter by manually inputting email addresses and sending to only 10 people at a time to prevent them bouncing back. Then technology advanced and along came the exciting day when I could do a proper, fully automated 'newsletter' to my entire list with one click of a button. You may laugh now, but twelve years ago this was very high tech and it liberated my marketing potential.

What a turning point. My ideas started to travel. I could share my techniques on how to shift and transform your life with all my clients. Everything I was sharing with clients in personal coaching sessions I could now take to a far broader audience. My tribe grew and grew and grew.

Next came a series of online courses to help support clients at a fraction of the one-to-one coaching investment. I was now using my writing to help shift clients around the world, and I loved the magic of global, leveraged potential.

I also started contributing articles regularly for magazines. I became the go-to expert on de-cluttering, living light and shifting your life. I was called on for my opinion in magazines, talk shows and live events. I wrote over 50 articles, penned 10 online courses and contributed a gazillion expert opinions in pretty much every one of South Africa's magazines, newspapers and radio/TV shows.

And then my business went to the next level.

In 2012, I was contemplating ways of growing globally and I suddenly got it into my head and heart that it was **Time to Write a Book**.

I also knew zip, nada, nothing about books or publishing whatsoever!

It was time for me (and my career) that I was seen to be 'credible' in a different way. I needed to see if a publishing house would agree to put their money where my big mouth was. I deeply believe in the power of synchronicity and following the threads that naturally unfold each step of the way. It requires trust and showing up—something I teach.

So the book was now in my space and I 'slapped' together some semblance of thoughts that naively became the start of my book proposal. I mentioned it to one or two people, and within a week an acquaintance said she knew a family-owned publishing house. She offered to introduce me to them.

A week later I was having coffee at 44 Stanley, a trendy spot in Johannesburg, and pitching my book idea to a publisher. (This is where my confidence, *chutzpah* and brand came in to play.)

My specific expertise was helping people clear their clutter. I had a body of work backed up with clients and references, an active platform, a voice, speaking engagements and a 'tribe' of followers. I told the publishers I knew I could help sell my books. Publishers need to know their risk is mitigated and they signed me as a new author, pretty much on the spot! They signed me based on a three-page book idea (the right idea at the right time) and a bucket load of contacts and confidence.

Clear Your Clutter was published in 2013 and my book launch was held on my 45th birthday. A highlight of my life. I even had my birthday cake made with the cover of my book on the icing. Next came *Ditch Your Glitch* in 2015. *Shift Your Home* was published in 2017 and 2nd Edition printed in 2018.

Becoming a published author had a very direct impact on the trajectory of my career path. Apart from the sheer fun of signing books at events, it gave me the opportunity to reach a larger audience and impact more lives around the world. One of my favorite 'kicks' is to engage with readers on one of the online forums or to receive an email with heartfelt thanks about how my books have shifted their lives.

SHOW UP FOR YOUR MESSAGE!

SHOW UP FOR YOUR BOOK!

SHOW UP FOR THE PLANET!

Now it is *your* turn, and this is how to get started on your dream! Set yourself up right to START STRONG and focus properly from the outset.

One of the biggest reasons why some writers manage to go all the way from finishing their first draft to actually publishing their books is simply because they followed these steps right from the start to SET UP STRONG. These steps, coupled with Sarah's RULES OF WRITING, will take you all the way. Step by step. This process of writing a book seeks to combine technical headspace exercises with heart- and soul-based exercises.

Before you move on to the next task, do your very best to SET YOURSELF UP within the next 24 hours.

Buy a notebook

Now it's time to go on a little adventure to your favorite book-store or stationers and have fun buying a writing notebook. This is the book you will use to plan, take notes and write exercises.

Choose a special notebook that delights you and begs you to write in it. It will be your trusted companion and confidant supporting you through this internal journey!

Whilst you are at it, perhaps it is time for a new pen?

Schedule your personal writing time NOW

We affectionately call this 'BUM TIME' on all our mentorships and retreats. And it literally means what it says ... you sit on your butt, glued to your chair! How are you practically going to carve out time to dedicate to your writing process over the next few months? I suggest that you block off specific time slots and make regular appointments with yourself right now. You might not know your preferred writing rhythm yet.

Perhaps it's an hour a day?

Or 90 minutes at dawn for three mornings a week?

Twice a week for four hours?

Seven hours solid on the weekend?

What works for you and your lifestyle?

I absolutely know that making appointments with yourself in your diary increases your odds of completing your book. Trust me on this one! You need non-negotiable time slots in your diary. It you have to give up a dedicated time slot for an emergency or a meeting then the rule is that you have to reschedule it. Immediately! If you had to cancel a hair appointment, would you honestly wait another six weeks for that trim or color? Not a chance in hell. You would immediately make another appointment. Apply the same rule to your writing.

This practice alone will set you apart from other writers who, with the best intentions in the world, never managed to complete their book. If you renege on this, you renege on your dream.

Schedule 'block time'

There is another deeper layer of bum time that we call 'retreat time' or 'block time'. This is about dedicating a long weekend or preferably a week to your precious book project. I suggest you do this in about four to five weeks' time when you are deeper into the writing process. Retreat/block time is all about removing yourself temporarily from your life, work, commitments and everything that usually pulls 'at' you and your energy. You will gift this time to yourself to totally immerse in your book. Block time is one of those magical book hacks that give you the edge. The trick is to pre-book and pay for it NOW. It can be a local trip just an hour away—or even in your own home if needs be. It can also be further afield (we run writing retreats in Greece, Spain, Italy, South Africa and the USA). Wherever it is, it does require you to intentionally and temporarily shut off from the rest of your world.

I have done some very successful home retreats. I tell my significant others and clients that I am not available, I cancel all social arrangements and I buy enough food so that I do not have to leave the house. And then I just get to it. So, if you cannot afford the time or money to get away, don't let that be your excuse for not completing this project.

What would you choose? A completed book or a list of excuses?

Make a dedicated book folder

I suggest that you create a 'book project' folder on your desktop for all book related documents for ease of retrieval. Your actual book will be written on one long Word document. Avoid the temptation to open a new folder or file for each chapter. You can keep ideas, inspirational pictures and research in your book folder. Keep it simple!

Go on a treasure hunt

Go on a quick treasure hunt with the sole purpose of gathering together any scattered notes, ideas, hastily scribbled words on Post-it notes, paper serviettes with pivotal reminders that have accumulated over the years, your journals, workbooks, PowerPoint presentations, talks, reports, pictures, photos and anything else pertaining to what you are writing about. Your treasure might be lurking in several different spaces but now it needs to be in ONE place.

If you are writing a subject-specialist book you are going to have to dig out records. Find things like processes, checklists, articles, newsletters, presentations, media clippings, and copies of talks that you have given. Get the toolkit of your trade together.

Prepare your writing space

Take the time to create a beautiful and inspirational writing space. This is about paving the way for your brain, energy, heart and creative juices by preparing your environment for effortless writing.

This could mean a few things for you:

- Shake it up a little bit
- A paper detox
- Clear the junk on your desk
- Shake it up a lot: we're talking a major desk and study overhaul.

Whatever you do, you deserve a space that makes you want to write—often!

When you are satisfied with your space, turn your attention to your computer. Give it a good physical clean (sticky keys are not conducive to writing), tidy up your desktop, clear out your inbox, and do some digital organizing. In short, make it as de-cluttered as possible so as not to distract you from your writing process. This is especially important for 'location-free' digital nomads or café writers like myself, who move around to different venues and do not have the same space to nestle into daily.

Get the right support

Writing is a solitary pursuit. But that's entirely necessary to complete your first draft. Just you and your ideas, notes and computer. On the other hand, there is huge value in having the right community of support who 'gets' you. One of the best ways to hold yourself accountable is to interact with our Facebook community. Our Facebook support group is for our group of writers only, so it's a safe space to share, commit and get feedback. The moment you request to join the group, you will be prompted on how to introduce yourself.

Join us here
https://www.facebook.com/groups/writein100days/

Get a writing buddy

If you're looking for something more intense, get an accountability partner. We call this your writing buddy. Our Facebook group is just that. We can pair you up with a buddy. A writing buddy will drastically improve your odds of finishing your project—especially when the going gets tough and you need an understanding and sympathetic ear, a nudge or a mighty shove.

You can meet up to write at a coffee shop if in the same city, help anchor each other to specific deadlines over email, or touch base via Messenger. Some writing buddies become lifelong friends and it's easy to see why.

Whatever you do, don't stay isolated. You will really battle to reach your goals.

TASK 4

Think Big! Why Your Book Needs a Single Big Idea

> 'Non-fiction requires enormous discipline. You construct the terms of your story, and then you stick to them.'
>
> **Barbara Kingsolver**

YOU START STRUCTURING A BOOK by being very clear on what you are writing about. Sounds simple?

You (sort of) know what you want to say and it feels logical to you, but how do you present it to the reader in a way that is clear, logical and compelling?

It's much harder than it sounds. Surely this book is about YOU? Or at least your story.

People often write to me and say … Sarah, I want to write a story about:

- ✓ My motor neuron disease
- ✓ My 20-year battle with bulimia
- ✓ My sex addiction
- ✓ My lessons learnt about money
- ✓ My gardening tips
- ✓ My adventure through Africa on a unicycle

- ✓ My 10 years as a stripper
- ✓ My father's harrowing organ harvesting in Cambodia.

And these are all great stories to write. But a book demands more of a writer than just noting down your thoughts, ideas or experiences. Because the hard truth is that most readers who will buy your book (with the exception of your friends and family) don't know you. That is why we took a look at a theme and tried to find one.

Your book needs to be elevated into something that speaks to the reader. That is why all books about you need to be about more than you. They need to be about something bigger than you.

Enter the realm of the Big Idea. All non-fiction books need one. Yes, just one.

What is this big idea?

The Big Idea is a single and clear statement that both positions you as an expert, and also answers the question: What is your book about?

You want to tell the reader the answer to this in the most obvious, clear, easy-to-understand and exciting way possible. You don't want to imply what it's about, or hint at it—you want to state it clearly, and upfront.

Most Big Ideas are stated (or contained) in the title, or at least on the cover of your book. We are going to get there, but let's just pin down some possible Big Ideas.

Sometimes the idea or topic seems obvious.

It's about your addiction.

Or your life.

Or it's a book about sales techniques ... Isn't it?

Well, no. That is not tight enough. That is not yet a Big Idea. That is still all about you.

A Big Idea does not just say, 'This is what my book is about', it also positions you in the debate. It puts a stake in the ground. It delivers an argument or a solution.

Look at all the book ideas below. All of them contain some argument. Most of them are quite radical or positional. They are not saying … this is a book about grief, or how to get rich. They are delivering a revolutionary or positional take on it.

- You can see grief as magic if you look right (*My Year of Magical Thinking* by Joan Didion)
- You can get filthy rich in two years (*How to Get Filthy Rich* by Mohsin Hamid)
- You need to change the way you think about money if you want to make it and keep it (*Rich Dad Poor Dad* by Robert Kiyosaki)
- Only 20? Time to learn to manage your money *Manage your Money like a Fu***ng Grownup* by Sam Beckbessinger)
- Little things can have big consequences (*The Tipping Point* by Malcolm Gladwell)
- You will lose weight/be healthier if you eat like this/like me. *This is basically the core argument of any diet book out there.*

In fact, I am going to take the Big Idea one step further – for non-fiction (NF) authors in particular.

Your Big Idea should:

✓ Be an argument or a solution
✓ Go against the current grain, offer a new idea, or give you an edge
✓ Be revolutionary, radical or a new take on something.

WRITING TASK

What's your Big Idea?

Boil down what your story is about into a single sentence of no more than five words. Go back to that theme you chose. That is a good place to start. Remember that this idea is about the book and NOT about YOU.

Aim for about three of these with different takes on your story.

Take it one step further. Turn your Big Idea into a position or argument.

Remember this: the Big Idea sometimes reveals itself in the writing of the book, so if it's elusive, don't let that derail your progress. It will emerge.

Your Big Idea checklist

- ✐ Is not about you, it is about the concept (or theme)
- ✐ It is single-minded
- ✐ It is tightly-focused
- ✐ It contains a universal message
- ✐ It contains a clear solution or argument (even if it is only really for you)
- ✐ It can be contained in a single sentence
- ✐ It is radical, revolutionary or disruptive.

Task 5
Find Your Genre

> 'We never end up with the book we began writing. Characters twist it and turn it until they get the life that is perfect for them. A good writer won't waste their time arguing with the characters they create ... It is almost always a waste of time and people tend to stare when you do!'
>
> **C.K. Webb**

THE VERY FIRST THING A literary agent or publisher will ask you is … what is your genre?

This doesn't mean that I want a breakdown of your plot. It means that I want to know what kind of book it is. Put simply, on which shelf do I stock it in a bookshop, or which section it will be loaded into on digital publishing platforms such as Amazon.

Genre drives book sales. When I ask 'What is your genre?' it is a one-sentence answer. Like: 'It is a travel memoir. It's a gluten-free cookbook. It's a personal finance advice book. It's a sports memoir. It's a business advice book.'

Not …

'Well, it's the story of my life. It is about love, and loss and family dramas.'

Nope. Beep.

It CAN be about that, but what's the genre?

Family memoir? Great!

Genre is a label that tells the reader what to **expect** in your book. It tells the booksellers how to **sell** your book. It also tells you, as an author, WHAT needs to be in your book to satisfy a reader.

It's really that simple. If you buy a book that promises you that you will lose weight, but it doesn't have a diet plan or even suggest what you should eat, you'd be pretty upset.

The first decision you will make when you decide on a genre boils down to this: Are you writing **fiction** (a novel) or **non-fiction** (a factual book)?

This workbook deals with non-fiction only. Writing a novel? Wrong book!

Non-fiction books fall under these big divisions:

- ✓ **Non-fiction:** This is any book that is based on facts (a 'how to' or a business book written by an expert or professional).
- ✓ **An autobiography:** This is a factual account of your life story.
- ✓ **A memoir:** This is an account of a section of your life, passed through the filter of memory.
- ✓ **A biography:** This is a factual account of someone else's life.

KEY POINT! Choosing your genre and understanding what a reader expects from a particular type of book is the first step in building a story that works. Your job as a writer is to be clear about where and how your book will be sold. You also need to know what a reader who loves your chosen genre will want and expect to find in your book.

WRITING TASK

You need to put a stake in the ground and choose a single, clear and publishable genre for your book.

1. Turn to List 2 in the Addendum

Start at List 2 and take a look at the non-fiction genres as categorized by Amazon.

Circle ALL the sections where you think your book could be listed.

Now reduce the list and choose only three genres that your book could be listed under.

2. Memoir writers, next look very carefully at List 3 in the Addendum. Find your particular book.

3. Visit a bookstore and get clear

- Where would your book sit in the store? (Remember, it can only sit on one shelf.)
- What books would be sold next to it?
- What do they have in common?
- How would yours be different?

Complete this statement and stick this in your notebook or on your writing wall

- I am writing a … (genre)
- It will be stocked on this shelf in my favorite bookstore …
- It will be listed in these two categories on Amazon …

HEART EXERCISE

Keep moving with speed through Part 1. Ideally, you are going to finish up to the end of TASK 11 within 10 days. TEN DAYS! This is your powerful preparation and planning time and it likes a dose of speed.

Are you on track or has life already gotten in the way?

Start these sentences in your journal and let your heart respond:

- Right now I am feeling ... about this process of writing
- What if my book …
- How can I possibly …
- I'm not sure that …
- I can keep going by …

📖 TASK 6

Do You Need To Be An Expert To Write?

> 'Writing non-fiction is more like sculpture, a matter of shaping the research into the finished thing. Novels are like paintings, specifically watercolors. Every stroke you put down you have to go with. Of course you can rewrite, but the original strokes are still there in the texture of the thing.'
>
> **Joan Didion**

HERE'S THE QUESTION THAT LURKS in the back of the mind of many writers … am I actually qualified to write a book?

The book could be about … making money, controlling diabetes, training a dog, losing weight, coping with grief. But am I qualified at all?

Good question. Do you have to be an authority to write a book? The simplest answer is YES!

Ask yourself this, would you read a book on managing your property written by someone who has never done it?

No! You need someone who's done it, knows the tricks and tells you how to do it too. In fact, you want more than that! You want them to bypass all their years of knowledge and just give you the gems. You want the shortcuts, the bits that matter. You want the roadmap.

You don't have to be a professional, but you DO have to have YOUR area of expertise. But this can be as small or big as you make it.

I like to categorize non-fiction/memoir writers into three types of experts:

- ✓ You're a **professional** expert or role model. This one is clear-cut. The assumption in these books is that you, as the author and expert, have the solutions. You're a chef, dietician, lawyer, pro-surfer, professional athlete, psychologist, or dog trainer, and you want to share your specific knowledge with others. Easy one. This can even extend into fun experts … money magic, dating consultants, sexperts. These books are straight-up non-fiction, and you can mix in your personal story.
- ✓ You are an expert of **lived experience**. You may not have studied professionally, or got a qualification in this, but you have lived this journey. Perhaps ... you had anorexia or ME for 15 years and you want to share your story. You cured your insomnia with magic mushrooms. You learned how to cope with the loss of a child. You walked the Great Wall of China barefoot. This is the domain of memoirs (less so of non-fiction). This type of expert is going to tell the reader their personal story and present their personal solutions.
- ✓ You are no expert at all, but you are going to do the **research and speak to experts**. You may be a professional or not, but you are going to look at what's out there and report back to your reader. Often these books start with a Big Idea and the writer—often a journalist—finds evidence to support that idea. The evidence can be formal or informal—which means interviews with friends! A biography would be a research book.

Why is it important to know what kind of authority you are?

- ✓ It determines how the publisher can sell your book and market you.
- ✓ It gives you a clear indication of your genre and what needs to be in your book.
- ✓ It helps you understand how you need to structure your book to lead the reader into your story and provide the information.

If you are an expert sharing personal or lived experiences you cannot offer professional solutions … only YOUR solution along with your journey. If you are a research expert you cannot offer your own solutions, only share what others (more qualified) found as a solution.

WRITING TASK

1. How are you qualified to write THIS book? How has your journey made you some sort of expert in what you are going to write about? Write this in the form of a paragraph, or you could expand this into a chapter, where you talk to your readers and set yourself up as qualified.

2. Now write a list of 10–30 lessons you have learned on this journey that you would like to share. This is a short and sharp point-form list—maximum one sentence per point.

3. Write a promise to your reader. This is a clear statement of purpose for yourself and your book. What is a reader going to get out of your book if they read it?

Is it going to … give them solutions, tell them a rocking story, reveal a crazy insider view into a secret life, drag them on a drug-fueled trip around the clubs of Singapore, deliver them a weight-loss journey, teach them how to code, or cook, or map out a sales plan?

Write up to 800 words in which you spell out, in detail, exactly what your book is going to offer the reader. Most often this can sit on the back cover, or in your first few chapters.

The One Minute Millionaire by Mark Victor Hansen and Robert G. Allen has a list on the back cover that tells a reader what they will learn from reading their book. Among these are:

- The power of one great idea
- How to develop multiple streams of income
- Six forms of leverage
- The essentials of marketing success.

'In every city, often behind the scenes, there are thousands of enlightened millionaires who acquire their wealth in innovative and honorable ways—and then give back to their communities. This book will show you how to become one of them … more quickly than you ever imagined.'

The promise of *The One Minute Millionaire*—as stated clearly by its authors—is that readers will quickly learn to become enlightened millionaires who can give back to their communities.

Rich Dad Poor Dad by Robert Kiyosaki promises on its back cover that it will:

- Explode the myth that you need to earn a high income to become rich
- Challenge the belief that your house is an asset

- Show parents that they can't rely on the school system to teach their kids about money.

TASK 7

How To Build a Book

> 'Writing a non-fiction story is like cracking a safe. It seems impossible at the beginning, but once you're in, you're in.'
> **Rich Cohen**

THE DIFFICULT THING ABOUT PLANNING a book is working out how to break down all the information in your head. Most often it feels as if there is a great mass of data swirling inside your brain. Perhaps it is your story, or your decades of work experience. Perhaps it is theory you teach or unpack.

The task now is to break down all of this into a series of chapters.

All books (even novels) start with the author making a working plan of how the story will unfold for the reader.

In a non-fiction title, you are going to group all your information into chapters, which become a good and well-organized Table of Contents (TOC). A TOC is critical to focus you as the writer, and it allows the reader to choose the chapters they want to read, and the ones they may want to skip.

Memoirs and biography have a different plotting structure to non-fiction books, and it's closer to the plot structure of a novel. You need to tell a story, so you will plot these books using scenes as the building blocks to a story rather than chapters. More about this in Task 8.

Types of non-fiction book structures you can use

Here are some examples of good structures for non-fiction storytelling. Can you choose one that works for your book?

A Chapter-Based Non-Fiction Book

All non-fiction books are organized into clear and logical chapters. Chapters should be descriptive and contain clear breakdowns of what information is in that chapter. Remember that readers may not read all the chapters. They read some in their entirety, dip into others briefly, or skip some.

For example:

- *A Brief History of Time, From the Big Bang to Black Holes* by Stephen Hawking
- *The Subtle Art of Not Giving a F**** by Mark Manson
- *The Tipping Point* by Malcolm Gladwell

A Thematic Structure

This attaches a higher/organizing concept to your structure. It can be a metaphor, poem or list. For example, if you are writing a yoga book, you may want to link your chapters to the 7 Chakras. If you are writing a sales book, you may want to link your chapters to the four quarters of a financial year. Travel memoirs may move from country to country. Think *Eat, Pray, Love* by Elizabeth Gilbert and how she grouped her story into three sections. This book has 108 chapters, reflecting the 108 prayer beads on a mala.

For example:

- *The Four Hour Work Week* by Timothy Ferris. This structured in four themes to emulate the title
- *The 5 Love Languages* by Gary Chapman. Although this is a list it also speaks to the theme of five, pointing to five fingers on a hand

A List Structure

Lists are another useful way of grouping your information.

For example:

- *The 5 People you will Meet in Heaven* by Mitch Albom
- *Ten Days that Shook the World* by John Reed
- *The 7 Habits of Highly Effective People* by Stephen R. Covey

A Workbook

Non-Fiction experts commonly use this structure. This structure mixes a personal story with actual exercises or things for readers to put into action to take the insights deeper and move them from point A to point B. This is what you are currently reading. All diet books are workbooks.

For example:

- *The Artist's Way* by Julia Cameron
- *Success Principles* by Jack Canfield
- *Clear Your Clutter* by Kate Emmerson
- *What Are You Hungry For? The Chopra Solution to Permanent Weight Loss, Well-Being, and Lightness of Soul* by Deepak Chopra

A Visually Driven (or Photography-Based) Book

Any book that includes strong visual material is in its own genre. This includes cookbooks and Angel cards. Again, your chapters and images need to reflect a theme, thread or story.

For example:

- *The French Kitchen* by Joanne Harris and Fran Warde
- *Sea Change* by Craig Foster and Ross Frylinck

A Chronological Structure (Memoir and Biography)

The most logical structure is to pick a point at which to start the story. Then you follow a clear and logical order of events. Often in a non-fiction or memoir the reader already knows how the story ends.

For example:

- *Seven Years in Tibet* by Heinrich Harrer
- *Dreams from my Father* by Barack Obama
- *The Diving Bell and the Butterfly* by Jean-Dominique Bauby
- *Get Me to 21* by Gabi Lowe

A Semi-Chronological Structure (Memoir and Biography)

You may want to include a scene where you remember something from your childhood and jump back to that time for a single scene, or seesaw between time zones or places. You may want to use this to build some drama or tension. Then you can jump to another memory where the stakes are high.

If you jump around a lot you may need to include a marker before each scene to locate the reader, for example, 'Alabama 1956' or 'New York 2012'.

For example:

- *A Long Way Gone* by Ishmael Beah
- *Many Lives, Many Masters* by Brian Weiss
- *The Glass Castle* by Jeannette Walls

A Blog or Diary-style Structure (Memoir and Biography)
You tell it as it happens. This can be in short blog-style posts or in longer posts as if written in an actual diary.

For example:

- *So Close, Infertile but Addicted to Hope* by Tertia Albertyn
- *The Diary of a Young Girl* by Anne Frank
- *My Guantánamo Diary: The Detainees and the Stories They Told Me* by Mahvish Khan
- *The Sober Diaries: How One Woman Stopped Drinking and Started Living* by Claire Pooley

Postcards or Letters (Memoir and Biography)
Carefully crafted letters between correspondents can tell a story and slowly and enticingly reveal a plot. These can be letters, emails, blogs, and tweets.

For example:

- *I Will Always Write Back – How One Letter Changed Two Lives* by Caitlin Alifirenka and Martin Ganda
- *Conversations with God* by Neale Donald Walsch
- *A Postcard Memoir* by Lawrence Sutin

What should a Table of Contents look like?

On the next page is a shortened example of a TOC from one of our writers, David Beattie. He wrote a business-to-business expert book: *The Expert Landlord: Manage Your Residential Property like a Pro.*

Introduction – Set Yourself up for Success

How to use *The Expert Landlord*

Chapter 1: You are a Landlord

A tale of two landlords, Landlord – a definition, know your why and Let's burst your bubble – why NOT to be a landlord

Chapter 2: Managing Your Own Property is Your Key to Property Investment Success

Should you do your own property management? Or should you outsource it? When to move on from self-management, Outsourcing your property management, How to choose your rental agent, When to move on from your rental agent, Making your decision, Property management – a definition

Chapter 3: It's a (people) Business

What is a business, making the landlord-tenant relationship work, your operational system and your framework for success

Chapter 4: Know the Rules

Acts guiding rentals, tenant and landlord rights, and the Rental Housing Tribunal

Chapter 5: How to Attract the Right Tenant

Defining your ideal tenant, setting your rent, preparing your property for prospective tenants, where to advertize, designing a successful ad, and tracking your results

WRITING TASK

What is the best way to organize your book in a logical and easy-to-read manner?

You may want to brainstorm this question as a mind map, or put it into a list or Excel spreadsheet.

Ask yourself …

- What is the logical order?
- What can clearly delineate the information for the reader?
- What is the best way to group the information?
- What is the most natural flow?
- How can I 'chunk' the material down into bite-sized pieces?

At the end of this process I would like to see your entire structure in a simple one- or two-page list. Non-fiction writers, this will be your TOC.

You are aiming for anywhere between 12–80 chapters. Take some time on this. As you work, you are going to expand this list by adding in what information should fit under which chapter. This will grow and change as you write.

Aim to complete this in no more than 1–2 hours. You know all this information, so don't get too stuck on how best to break it down.

Memoir writers, please read Task 8 before you do this.

TASK 8

Tackle Your Book Scene By Scene, Chapter By Chapter

> 'They start with a simple premise and proceed logically, and inevitably, toward a conclusion both surprising and inevitable.'
>
> **David Mamet**

MEMOIR WRITERS, YOU NEED TO take a different approach to plotting than writers tackling a straight non-fiction title.

When you plan a memoir or biography, you tell your story in moments or dramatic scenes. You cannot narrate your entire story or life, so you need to select key moments from your life that dramatize the journey. So, if you are telling a story of your mother's battle with dementia, you are going to find those key events or moments that tell her story.

You may jump decades ahead at times. You may leave out huge parts of your life. Is your story about your child's lymphoma? Then perhaps it starts a few days before the diagnosis and travels that tight journey.

The key to memoir planning is to choose which scenes (or stories) you want to include and which you need to leave out … possibly for another book.

You build a memoir (and many non-fiction books) using scenes, not chapters.

Scenes are the smaller moments that, taken together, build the story.

This means you are telling your story in a series of events, each one illustrating the larger story.

- ✓ Each scene (event) functions as its own small story and has a beginning, middle and end.
- ✓ Each scene is short and self-contained. But it drives your story forward
- ✓ Driving your story forward means it needs to end with the reader wanting to know … what happened next?
- ✓ Each scene will be full of detail and color as if the reader is in your shoes and living your life
- ✓ Time is not always important. You can jump decades ahead, or choose all your scenes over a period of a few hours.

Aim for a list of between 50–80 key scenes. You can group three to five scenes into a chapter.

A rough memoir outline/scene list looks something like this:

- ✓ I meet Mark during the riot
- ✓ The proposal on the beach, we fall overboard
- ✓ Our first anniversary night, he looks ill
- ✓ Over two weeks he gets worse
- ✓ The first doctor's visit
- ✓ We find out I am pregnant, Mark collapses
- ✓ The doctor tells us Mark's diagnosis.

All scenes need to drive your story forward, but you may need some scenes that 'set the scene'.

These could be:

- ✓ Scenes that introduce a character, a house, a family
- ✓ Scenes that introduce the era, location or political context
- ✓ You do not have to connect the scenes. If you select them well

they will tell a logical story without you having to explain
- ✓ You may want a scene that covers an entire lifetime/career in order to set that person up.

Non-fiction (Nf) Writers

As you start to write, you will notice you need to expand your TOC or chapter list. You are going to progressively break your chapters down into smaller content buckets using subheadings or text boxes. This is because a chapter needs structure. It is not a long and rambling diatribe.

In non-fiction, these buckets or sections that make up each chapter may be elements such as:

- ✓ Personal sharing of your own story
- ✓ Client anecdotes
- ✓ A list of tips
- ✓ Research
- ✓ A box with case studies
- ✓ A section with your lessons
- ✓ A section with someone's (good or bad) advice
- ✓ Other people's stories, letters, emails, interviews
- ✓ A task lists for your reader
- ✓ Exercises for your reader
- ✓ An 'in a nutshell' chapter summary.

It is also a good idea to try to keep your structure consistent. This means in every chapter your reader expects to see the same structure.

WRITING TASK

Your task (NF) for today is to revisit your book structure and expand it. Create a far more detailed breakdown of how the chapters will work in your TOC.

Memoir writers, you will refine and revisit your scene list and grow it to between 50–80 scenes. Make sure that you number them.

Are you doing this on Excel? Or do you prefer record cards or Post-it notes that you can stick on your wall and move around? Find a method that suits your thinking and creative style.

Sarah says:

I find Excel easy to use as I can expand it and add extra rows and move things around on the screen.

Kate says:

I am more visual and love colorful, sticky post-it notes to put up on the wall or in a journal that I can shift around, as I need to. Excel stifles me.

TASK 9

What Type of Book Is Yours?

> 'Sometimes you read a book and it fills you with this weird evangelical zeal, and you become convinced that the shattered world will never be put back together unless and until all living humans read the book.'
>
> **John Green, *The Fault in Our Stars***

YOU HAVE ESTABLISHED YOUR GENRE—now how will your book play out in terms of how you present the information? A lot of this is a choice you must make upfront.

Most non-fiction books fall into one of two broad categories.

A how-to book

The key to this book is:

- ✓ You have done something/know something/learned something
- ✓ You are going to share with your readers how you did it and perhaps how they can do it too.

You can share this through your own personal story (memoir) or reveal it in a more step-by-step process that teaches the reader how to do something, such as how to be a better lover, leader, parent or dog owner.

To write a HOW TO book you have to be an expert in something, which means you have to have done it yourself. It helps if you are a professional expert in your chosen field.

It offers:

- ✓ Solutions
- ✓ Your personal story interwoven with the process.

Imagine these fields:

- ✓ Cookbook
- ✓ Diet book
- ✓ Sales book
- ✓ Tax law for small businesses
- ✓ Fitness guide
- ✓ Personal finance
- ✓ Workbook
- ✓ E-course
- ✓ Clearing your clutter.

A big idea book

This book has one central blatant idea, solution, argument or angle. You tell the reader what it is right upfront at the beginning hook of the book (and usually in the title too). The book is then walking the borders of this idea and exploring it and proving it.

You do not have to be an expert to write one of these. You do need a great angle or Big Idea, for example:

- *Fat in the Head: It's Not food That Makes you Fat It's How you Think* by Nina Frank and Natalie Uren
- *The Four Hour Work Week: Escape the 9–5, Live Anywhere and Join the New Rich* by Timothy Ferriss
- *LayGuide: How To Become the Ultimate Pick-Up Artist* by Tony Clink

Memoirs will also fit into these categories.

A memoir needs:

- ✓ A big central idea
- ✓ To tell or show the reader something you did or experienced
- ✓ A link to a bigger vision, solution or lesson (the Big Idea).

Expert non-fiction

You need to be an expert or professional practitioner of some sort to write this. You could be a sales expert, business or life coach, yoga teacher, car mechanic, businessman, or shaman. The difference here with a non-expert is important; you are sharing your story but you are also sharing processes, techniques, recommendations or solutions to the 'layman'. This can be a workbook or a straight non-fiction book.

For example:

- *The Dukan Diet* by Dr Pierre Dukan
- *How to Win Friends and Influence People* by Dale Carnegie
- *You Can Heal Your Life* by Louise Hay

Business-to-business / expert-to-professional

This is when an expert in a particular field is writing for other professionals in the field. This may cover how to improve your professional expertise and develop your continued professional development (CPD).

For example:

- *Hacking Marketing: Agile Practices to Make Marketing Smarter, Faster, and More Innovative* by Scott Brinker

- *Content Inc.: How Entrepreneurs Use Content to Build Massive Audiences and Create Radically Successful Businesses* by Joe Pullizi

WRITING TASK

Where does your Big Idea start? It starts with your title.

I know that when I walk into a bookstore, or click onto Amazon, the very first thing I browse is the title. Perhaps also the cover image. The moment the title grabs my attention, I may then read a little further, turn the book over and read the back blurb. But if the title doesn't speak to me, I probably won't spend a moment further on that book.

Do you find that is how you buy books too?

A title is stupidly the single biggest thing that sells a book. Crazy, right? All that work you put into writing it and people actually do judge a book by its cover.

We want you to come up with a good one. But without totally freaking out about it yet. Trust us, it will get better by the end of this process.

You need a working title. Something that frames your idea and holds it all together. You may already feel attached to ONE favorite title already, but today you get to play around a bit.

Brainstorm 20 different titles for your book. Yep, 20! Don't stop until you have 20. Chances are that down the line your publisher (or you) will not choose the one you currently feel is best. Having options is important. Get creative, serious, wacky, funny, and outrageous. Please make sure at least five titles are humorous.

The title of Kate's first book, *Clear Your Clutter* was actually the 17th one on her list. Definitely not her favorite and yet it became a bestseller. Go figure!

PS … You don't need anything fancy and if you are stuck you can call it '*My Gripping Story*'.

HEART EXERCISE

Take a little play-time now and create a dream cover for your book.

Take your favorite current working title, your author name and an image that captures the essence of your book. Start playing around with what you imagine the cover might look like. Perhaps take some pictures from the internet, or from magazines, or just draw it out if you have creative flair. Maybe it's in PowerPoint or just a fun, simple scribble on a piece of paper. If you love the pull of visuals, but aren't that great at making them, you could go one step further and get a designer friend/freelancer to rustle something up for you.

This process of creating your cover is designed to get your subconscious working, magnetizing you forward and inspiring your commitment to completion.

When you have created your cover, stick it up on your wall where you write, for visual stimulation, make it a screen cover on your phone, or put it on your fridge.

We did this process ourselves with our writers in Greece last year. We drew a mock-up for our cover, whilst gazing out at the blue Aegean. Then a year later when we actually started working on this book more seriously, there it was to inspire us to get it done. And now it is in your hands. The title is different, the stucture is different, but the seed was planted with that drawing in our hands.

Task 10
Where Are You Headed?

> 'You can fix anything but a blank page.'
> **Nora Roberts**

WHERE ARE YOU GOING WITH all this writing? Well, you are mostly likely shooting for a minimum of 50,000 typed words. Why 50,000? It is the minimum word count for a book with a spine that can sit on a shelf in a bookstore.

We are going to ask you to track your progress using word counts, not pages or chapters.

A chapter is anywhere from 1,500 words and upwards. This depends on how many chapters you want. There can be between 12–80 chapters in your book. This is your choice.

Do the maths! If your book is going to be 80,000 words and you have 10 chapters, you will need 8,000 words a chapter, right? That's a lot of information per chapter and perhaps too much.

- ✓ You may want to increase to 12–15 chapters and reduce your word count to 5,000 per chapter.
- ✓ Or would the information work better if your book had 38 chapters, each around 2,000 words?

Your only goal here during these 100 Days is to simply write your first draft of your book. Did we mention that?

What is a first draft? Well, it is simply the very first version of your book. And many authors will tell you that's the hard part. Getting your story out of your head and onto paper without self-editing too much is the challenge most writers face. But until you have a first version written down, you have nothing to work with. The story is still in your head, and yours alone. You have nothing to make better, smarter, tighter or more readable.

Does this mean you will have finished your book by the end of this process and it is ready to find a publisher? Not a chance. Most writers end up rewriting around five versions, iterations or drafts of any book before they send it to publishers. This first draft is often called a 'shitty first draft' because the truth is that most first versions of any writing project are just a rough assembly. You are most often never going to show THAT version to anyone. You are going to take it by the scruff of its neck, and do a second (better) draft. Sarah's Rules of Writing (Task 11) are the keys to getting it done. The first draft is what matters at this point!

You could even hand it over and allow an editor to make it better.

Sarah says

As a book editor I work on a lot of author's books to make them better. Sometimes they are great to begin with, and all I can do is just make them a bit tighter or clearer. Other times I can see that the author (or their publisher) has sent me their first version. Most often I will send that version back with a few pages of notes and a request for them to rewrite it one more time! Any agent or publisher can see a first version a mile off. I have made that mistake myself, getting so excited that I had finished my first novel that I wasted no time. I printed out some copies and posted (yes, posted, as I'm talking about the days before you submitted online) it off to the biggest publishers in the business. Needless to say, the rejection letters came just as fast.

So, we are working here to get your first draft only. This is the first step all writers must walk on the journey to publication.

Look ahead! These are the longer steps in your exciting writing journey ahead.

- ✓ **Step 1:** Get clear on your genre, story and tackle all the planning (10 days max)
- ✓ **Step 2:** Bash out your first draft (anywhere from 90 days to a year)
- **Step 3:** Take a bit of a break (a month minimum). You can start building your author brand at this stage
- ✓ **Step 4:** Start shifting into the publishing phase. Read through, then rewrite your second (better) draft (two weeks)
- ✓ **Step 5:** Craft your book one last time (your 3rd, 4th or 7th draft)! Max two weeks per version
- ✓ **Step 6:** Prepare all those pesky documents (Pitch Deck) you need to submit a book to a publisher (take a month)
- ✓ **Step 7:** Send it out to at least 20 publishers. Cry a bit. Want to give up …
- ✓ **Step 8:** Wait for up to a year, and keep sending while you wait. Writing a book is not a passing fancy. It is a Big Thing. If it's just a whim, well then you may quit after about 20,000 words when you realize what it really takes. It takes tenacity, perseverance and staying power. If you have picked up this book, you are writing more than just a series of blog posts. You are in for the long haul—the delight of a first draft!

Writing a book is a calling and if you hear the calling you will walk the entire path to the end. Don't give up on any of these steps.

The danger? You get into a loop of perfecting your first few chapters for years and never get beyond those.

The solution? To trust us and the process you are following in this book. You dive in, put your judgements aside and keep writing until you reach your WORD GOAL.

Ask yourself

What do you want to write? Get clear! Is it a book or something else?

It could be a:

- ✓ Full-length book: 50,000–80,000 words
- ✓ E-book: 10,000–50,000 words
- ✓ E-course
- ✓ An essay: 1,500 words
- ✓ A blog: 300 words
- ✓ A speech: 2,000–4,000 words
- ✓ A TED talk: 4,000 words
- ✓ An article: 1,500 words
- ✓ A personal essay: 3,000 words
- ✓ An academic paper
- ✓ A letter
- ✓ A journal
- ✓ A record for yourself or family.

WRITING TASK

Get clear! In a nutshell, what is your book about? Imagine that this is what will appear on the back cover of your book. It will tell a reader what to expect and what the content of the actual book is.

- Take a look at your bookshelf to inspire you and to see how other writers do this
- This should be three to five sentences
- This needs to be what you will say when someone asks you … what's your book about?

  Write a few versions and see which works best.

HEART EXERCISE

Commit to your writing deadline now!

You need a writing goal to complete your first draft. So, what is your SPECIFIC commitment for the end of this process? If you have taken the suggested 10 days for all the planning thus far, imagine yourself another 90 days down the line, mark the specific date in your diary and create your writing goal.

All writers working through this book, and our online mentorships, start with this end goal in mind. A clear and challenging goal you are aiming for. You need to know where you are headed, and actively work towards a completed first draft is the primary goal. If you already have a lot of written material, please stretch yourself and consider completing Parts 3 and 4 of this book too—starting to create your author brand, writing a second draft and your proposal.

Be clear, concise and focused:

- I commit to completing my first draft by …
- I commit to writing 60,000 words of my first draft
- By XYZ, I have finished my first draft and created a website.

- I am thrilled to have my first draft plus a book proposal in hand
- By the … I'll send off my first draft to … (my buddy, coach) for accountability.

HINT – What's the title of this book you're reading right now? It is possible to complete your whole book in 100 days. That's 10 days, planning and 90 days of writing. Of course, you can also take a year if you choose. But memoir and non-fiction also appreciate a bit of speed in the writing process. You want to get in, dive deep, immerse yourself and then get out and edit like a boss.

We don't suggest you let it linger (and potentially fester) for too long. Now that you have taken the step to buy this book, it's time to just DO IT! You have to trust yourself and us on this one, and pick the end date now.

Task 11
Sarah's Rules of Writing

> 'Write as freely and rapidly as possible and throw the whole thing on paper. Never correct or rewrite until the whole thing is down. Review in process is usually found to be an excuse for not going on. It also interferes with flow and rhythm which can only come from a kind of unconscious association with the material ...'
>
> **John Steinbeck**

THERE IS NO RIGHT OR wrong way to write a book, but after working with writers for over 15 years to get them published, I do have some rules that I know work. Read them! Stick them up! Use them!

Rule 1 – Know thy genre

Don't dare start until you are very, very clear about where your book sits on Amazon's list of genres. Go back to that Task 5 now if you are not yet 100% clear.

Rule 2 – Stick to a basic word editor

Close down all other programs every single time you sit down to write. The only program open must be Word (or Pages on a Mac). No email, no internet and definitely no Facebook. Try not to use fancy word-processing packages like Scrivener. They are just distractions, unless this is a program you already know well.

Rule 3 - Write an entire scene in one sitting

It takes a while to get into a scene (or section). You will fidget, move stuff around, make coffee, weed the garden, make toast, and reread your notes. The good material comes once you have got this out the way. Don't break your flow once you find it.

Rule 4 - Don't discuss your book with anyone until your draft is finished

Talking is not writing. Instead of telling people your stories, your challenge is now to move them into the written form. This rule is also to keep your own project sacred. You will find that everyone is 'writing a book'. Well YOU are doing it, so there is no need to talk about it.

Rule 5 - No self-editing or revising the previous day's work

This is the single most important rule that will get you to the end of your book. It is also one of the hardest to follow! Don't look back. Once you start writing, do NOT read your previous day's work. Just keep moving forward until you have finished the entire first draft. Your aim is to get your word count up. You will end up changing most of it in your second draft anyway.

Rule 6 - Do not read books similar to yours for the entire duration of your writing process

Your book is not unique. There are millions of books out there. You are bringing your own voice and life to an age-old story. Reading others' work will confuse you and make you judge your own story. You will want to write like them. Avoid this.

Rule 7 - Be clear about your book and chapters (or scenes) before you write

Don't start until you have (most of) your scenes roughly plotted so you understand the arc and flow of your story. If you are at this point in this book, you should have already worked through all of that by now!

Rule 8 - Don't change your story

There will come a time when you wonder why on earth you chose this story, this angle, when there are so many better ones out there. Well, there are not better ones, only distractions. This is your story—tweak, refine and improve—but stick with it to the end of your first draft.

Rule 9 - There is no such thing as writer's block

Really. Take my word for it. Writer's block only kicks in when you have been given a massive advance to write your 7th novel and you have no ideas. You might realistically be unsure, scared, confused, bored, irritated, usually fearful of what writing will require of you, but no, not blocked! Get rid of that excuse right now.

Rule 10 -There is no such thing as good or bad writing

I can't stress this enough. It is not the most talented writers who get published. It is the most disciplined and tenacious writers who get published.

Your writing style is your own. You will find readers who enjoy it, or an editor who can clean it up later.

Rule 11 - There is nothing you can't fix in a rewrite or second draft

This really speaks to Rule 5. That's why I don't want you to edit or revise your work each time you sit down to write. Leave it for the second draft.

I have worked with writers on many books so I also know that sometimes I have to throw the rules out the window. A recent writer who got a publishing deal spent eight years writing about her adventure in Tibet. She crafted, tweaked and slowly got the book written. A businessman last year threw his book together in four months using an Excel spreadsheet and a research assistant who gathered the facts. Some books only come together in the editing phase, or your best idea comes once the publisher has already sent your book off to the printers.

WRITING TASK

Copy these rules and stick them up above your writing space—or in your journal. When in doubt go back to them and take them to heart! Every one of them matters and sticking to them will get you to the end of your first draft!

HEART EXERCISE

We are all motivated by powerful and compelling quotes or sayings, which support, energize and inspire us. When life's demands run high, energy gets low, your fingers get tired and you are wondering what on earth to write to add the next 200 words, let alone two full scenes—you need a little boost.

Choose a quote that sums up your WHY, your bigger picture and the very reason for doing this. It needs to feel like a magnet pulling you forward. It could also be your favorite life quote—the essence of who you are and why you do what you do. It can be really useful to find a quote or phrase that is unique to THIS book and THIS project at THIS specific time in your life.

Write it out and stick it up in the space where you write.

Tomorrow you move on from planning and start writing.

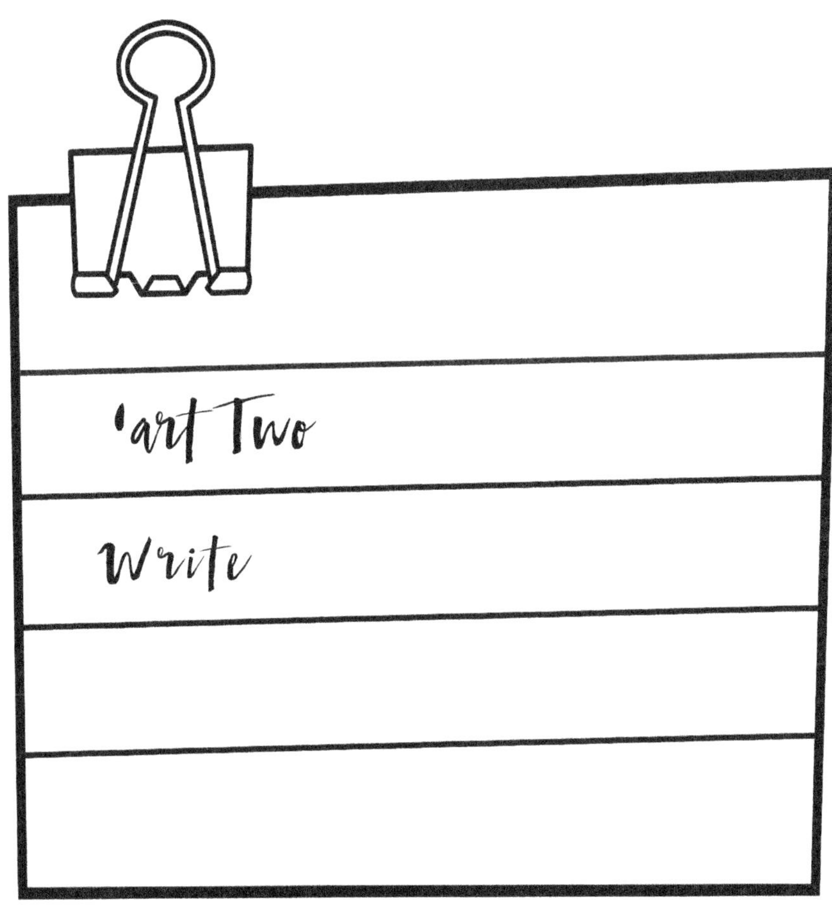
'art Two
Write

> 'I think we ought to read only the kind of books that wound and stab us.'
> **Franz Kafka**

WE ARE NOW SHIFTING GEAR. You are a bit clearer about what you are writing and why, your genre and your rough book plot or structure.

From now on your only real task is to start writing and to keep writing until you hit your word count. Remember that you are aiming for a minimum of 50,000 words in the next 90 days. Is your writing commitment written out and stuck up?

Please look at the Word Count Tracker in the Addendum. You are going to use this to check on your progress after every writing session. It will help you set goals and targets to get you to the end. We suggest you photocopy this and stick it up on your writing wall or in your notebook.

TASK 12

Hook Them from The Start

> You can't wait for inspiration, you have to go after it with a club.'
>
> **Jack London**

WHERE SHOULD YOUR STORY START? Few stories start at the beginning. Most stories start in the middle.

All stories—whether it's a novel, short story, children's story, picture book, magazine article or screenplay—start with something happening. We call this the inciting incident.

You HAVE to start with a Big Bang. Hook them!

- ✓ In a crime novel the inciting incident is almost always the actual murder, or the discovery of a body.
- ✓ In an action novel the book starts with a terrifying act, a murder, or a sense of foreboding about an approaching disaster.
- ✓ In a romance you would start with the heroine meeting the hero.

This inciting incident is indispensable because it is the HOOK. Your opening chapter needs to hook your reader and draw them into your story. It needs to make them want to keep reading.

The inciting incident – the Hook – is the spark that ignites your book.

In a memoir or non-fiction book you have to find that event from your own life or your subject's life. You are looking for a dramatic moment to start your story.

In non-fiction equally, your first scene often needs to be personal, dramatic and engaging. It starts the inquiry (story) or argument that your book will explore over the next few thousand words. This scene also needs to **set up your book**. It needs to pose a problem and lots of questions, and the promise to answer them all.

It could be:

- ✓ The lowest point of your story
- ✓ The start of it all
- ✓ A client encounter
- ✓ The time of your biggest questioning
- ✓ A hilarious encounter
- ✓ A dramatic event or moment
- ✓ The moment that alters your life forever
- ✓ The day you get your diagnosis/news/retrenchment.

Brandon Bays' *The Journey* starts with her walking into a doctor's office with a basketball-sized tumor.

Anita Moorjani's *Dying to be Me* starts with the chapter: 'The Day I Died'.

Elizabeth Gilbert's *Eat, Pray, Love* starts with the protagonist (Liz) lying awake, knowing she is going to leave her husband the next day.

Anthony Robbins' *Notes from a Friend* starts with a story of young boy in a dirt-poor family with no food for Thanksgiving. That boy was him and a gift that day changed his life.

Writers often ask me:

- ✓ Why do we even have inciting incidents?
- ✓ Who says there even has to be something dramatic at the start?
- ✓ Can't I just plunge in and start the story when I was a child?
- ✓ Doesn't the story start all by itself?

The truth is that readers (you included) give a book a very limited time to prove itself. You pick it up, read the first chapter, and if the book doesn't really grab you—well, then you put it down.

So as a writer you do want to find the most compelling place to start your book. You need to understand that the start of your book is a SET UP.

Ask yourself:

- ✎ What is an exciting way to start THIS story?
- ✎ What moment in time can draw the reader in?
- ✎ Is it specific?
- ✎ Is it personal?
- ✎ Does the way I start this book set up or tease my reader into my bigger story?

List at least five dramatic events, moments or stories that need to be in your book or story.

After answering these questions, you will write your opening scene NOW.

End it in a long series of questions. This may feel stupid.

However, you need to spell out the issues you are grappling with in a straightforward way so both you, and your reader, are clear about the journey.

How could this happen to me?
How did I lose my business?
How could I not have noticed his betrayal?
How can I change this?

Done your start? Now move on with your writing and don't look back.

HEART TASK

Write a few sentences on each of these:

- Why this?

(Why this message? Why do people need to hear OUR voice?)

- Why me?

(Why not someone more experienced? Why do YOU need to tell this story?)

- Why now?

(Why today? Why not tomorrow? Why not next year?)

TASK 13

What Do You Need to Give Up to Finish?

> 'Perfection is not when there is no more to add, but no more to take away.'
>
> **Antoine de Saint-Exupéry**

WRITING YOUR BOOK WILL REQUIRE that you make some shifts in your life. Say yes to some things and no to others. As a life coach, I want to address the topic of BOUNDARIES. You will have to shift away from life's frequent requests, obligations, and demands, as well as any projects that will pull at your energy. You will definitely have to implement some healthy boundary lines to be able to complete your first draft. One of the hardest jobs you will encounter is to manage your own distractions and internal procrastination tricks, followed very closely by managing everyone else doing the same to you.

You can rarely expect someone else to say: 'Hey there, I'll do X for you today so you can write some more.'

As much as that would be wonderful, and it may miraculously happen to you, you also have to muster up the courage to say no, and ask for the additional support you need right now in your home or work environment. When thinking about the topic of boundaries, it helps to remember that your writing project has a fixed timeline, and it is not forever. When I wrote my second book, *Ditch Your Glitch,* the deadline was an extremely tight two months down the line. Every time anyone invited me for coffee, dinner, or to a new potential client meeting—if it wasn't something that was absolutely 100% essential—my standard response was: 'I would love to, but I am currently on a very tight deadline, so please get hold of me after the 31st March when my time frees up again.'

BAM! Boundaries in place, no one pulling me off task, and I made sure I met my tight deadline for my publisher. It requires not caring what others think of you. It requires tenacity and strength of character. You don't even have to tell anyone what the deadline is that you are working towards—just the word deadline carries enough gravitas. Don't feel like you need to over-explain anything. Be clear and get back to your writing tasks.

You have to be willing to dig deep, give up certain things, and give yourself permission to achieve your own deadline. It is tough writing on your own, which is why so many writers bail on their own process, or get stuck in the loop of writing their first draft forever and a day. It is also why many writers join us on our international retreats or online mentorships to ensure 200% commitment and make it non-negotiable.

While you remember in Sarah's Rules of Writing we say that you should not tell people about your book, it can be useful to have a writing buddy—or use our Facebook group for that support. Having someone else helps you stay accountable to your own goal, and helps you keep going when the going gets tough. We all need help along the way—or we will just give in to procrastination and everything else that may come along to hijack our writing project.

HEART EXERCISE

What do you specifically need to renegotiate, push back on or creatively rearrange to go to the next level with your writing? What do you need to reach your 50,000 word mark in 100 days?

Look ahead to your own deadline, and mark a celebratory gathering in your calendar now. That way when people want or need to see you, you can tell them you will be coming out of the heavy workload on THAT date. You can celebrate your completed first draft milestone, so you don't feel like you are missing out on too much socially!

Challenge to give something up!

Chances are your life and calendar are already pretty full with commitments, engagements, hobbies and projects on top of family and work life. You are no different from any other writer. Less than 1% of writers working on a book are doing it full time! So the real question becomes 'what are you going to GIVE UP in order to release that time and energy for your book?'

You might have to forego a couple of hours of TV every night, or one social gathering with the girls, or that game of squash with the lads. While I advocate a balanced life that requires physical exercise and plenty of interaction with loved ones, you might realistically need to reprioritize things for a while. It might involve getting shared lifts to school for your kids, or saying no to requests to get involved in events or charities for the next couple of months. I always find it useful to tune out a lot more from social life and social media when on a writing deadline.

What do YOU have to willingly adjust and give up in order to GIVE MORE energy to your book? You need to be specific on this one and make that commitment now. It's a good idea to share this if on the Facebook group, as it will add another layer of accountability.

TASK 14
Where Is Your Book Set?

> 'My valley, the Swat Valley, is a heavenly kingdom of mountains, gushing waterfalls and crystal-clear lakes. Welcome to Paradise it says on a sign as you enter the valley.'
>
> **Malala Yousafzai, *I Am Malala***

WHERE IS YOUR STORY ACTUALLY taking place? Readers will want to walk into this world with you.

The **setting** is the physical world in which all your action is going to take place. You have to build this world and make it real. You are inviting your reader to step into this world for a bit. It is your job to locate your reader and make the actual setting come alive. In a novel we call this WORLD BUILDING. But it is equally important in a memoir and a non-fiction book to create a tangible and real world so that your characters are not floating nowhere (or anywhere) in the universe.

You want your reader to know that you are in:

- ✓ Wall Street, 1999 – *The Wolf of Wall Street* by Jordan Belfort
- ✓ Swat Valley, Pakistan – *I Am Malala: The Girl Who Stood Up for Education and Was Shot by the Taliban* by Christina Lamb and Malala Yousafzai
- ✓ Montecito, California, 2004 – *My Life in France* by Julia Child

- ✓ A dark basement under your house – *The Imam's Daughter* by Hannah Shah

Ask yourself:

- ✓ Which are the locations you want to take your reader to?
- ✓ What can you leave out?
- ✓ How important is the setting and how much attention must you give it?
- ✓ How big (a city) or small (a coffee shop) do you want to go?
- ✓ Is your location an era, city, house, company culture or hospital?

Choose a few settings to really develop and make them come alive using:

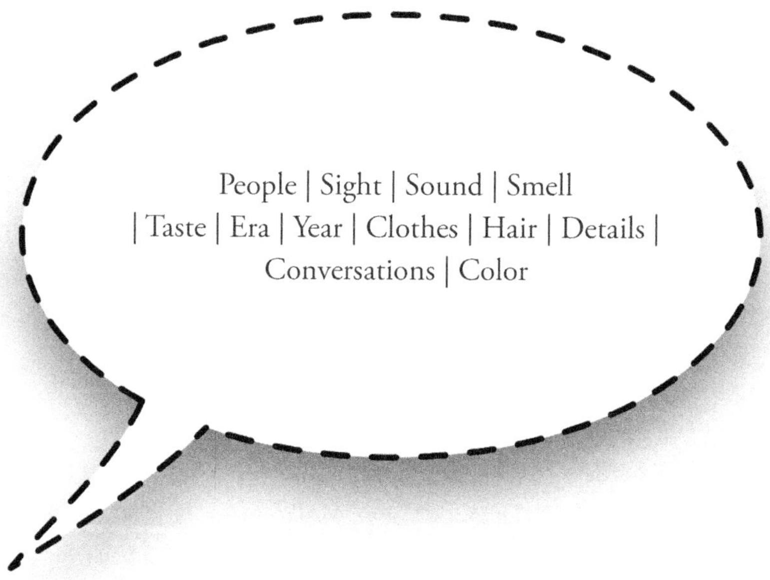

WRITING TASK

I want you to write a scene in which you build a location. Be very specific and describe a key location in your story. It could be any setting – often your home city is a good one.

In *I am Malala*, Mahala uses an entire chapter to set up the beauty of Pakistan and explain the history, culture and religion.

Take your reader on a walk into your world. Use some history, draw in some color. Make it come alive.

YOUR WORD COUNT TARGET IS 5,000 WORDS

TASK 15

The Hero – That's You!

> 'No one wants to read about characters who are just anybody. They want to read about interesting somebody's, characters capable of evoking in the reader some measure of emotional response.'
>
> **James N. Frey**

A BOOK WITHOUT A HERO is a like a movie without a star. Even if that hero is you. In fact, in non-fiction and memoir the hero IS YOU.

How do you describe yourself to your reader in a way that is real, authentic and relevant? How do you make yourself, as the narrator and lead character, come alive? You need to pour yourself on to the page, even if you are a reluctant hero.

So who is your hero (even if it's you)? Are you?

abusive	cynical	impatient	obsessive
active	decisive	impulsive	optimistic
adventurous	determined	independent	outgoing
affectionate	direct	intelligent	patient
aggressive	domineering	introvert	persistent
ambitious	easy-going	rational	pessimistic
annoying	emotional	reliable	pompous
anxious	enthusiastic	reserved	practical
artistic	energetic	ruthless	serious
bossy	extroverted	sarcastic	shy
brave	fearful	secretive	sincere
calm	frank	self-centered	sociable
cautious	friendly	selfish	stubborn
charming	funny	sensible	superficial
cheerful	generous	sensitive	tactful
compulsive	gentle	lazy	tactless
confident	greedy	loyal	thoughtful
conservative	gregarious	mean	untrustworthy
courageous	gullible	modest	witty
cowardly	happy	moody	wise
creative	honest	nervous	zany
cruel	imaginative	nice	zealous

The hero checklist for memoir writers (it's all about you!)

Eye color:
Hair color:
Haircut/style:
Hair length:
Coloring/features:
Height:
Best feature:
Worst feature:
Attractive on a scale of 1–10:
Personality flaw:
Personality in a nutshell:
Physical quirk:
One odd habit:
Star sign:
Worst characteristic and trait:
Personal motto:
What drives you?
What are you very, very good at?
What do you hate the most?
Something you are?
Something you aren't?
Melody you always hum?
Three words that describe you:
Bad mood mode:
How would someone realize you are irritated or impatient?
One thing kept with you at all times:

Readers read books for the story but also for intimacy—they want to move into a character's life, live inside his or her thoughts and emotions, and take on his or her goals and problems.

We will work on YOU as the hero of your memoir on a deeper level later in this book.

WRITING TASK

You are going to include a scene in which you describe yourself in a very tangible and physical way. By the end of the scene we want to know if we would recognize you if you walked into the room.

Here is how Jordan Belfort did it in his memoir *The Wolf of Wall Street*:

'Unlike Scott, I don't look like a goldfish, which made me feel proud as he stared at me, searching my face for irony. I'm on the short side, though, and at the age of twenty-four I still had the soft boyish features of an adolescent. It was the sort of face that made it difficult for me to get into a bar without getting proofed. I had a full head of light brown hair, smooth olive skin, and a pair of big blue eyes. Not altogether bad-looking.'

Use one of these triggers to describe yourself

- ✐ I looked into my reflection and leaned closer …
- ✐ Other people say I am …
- ✐ I adjusted my (clothing) and looked down ...
- ✐ I caught him looking at me. I know I am …

Read this scene out to someone you trust.

Memoir writers, answer these questions:

- Where are you when we meet you at the start?
- Why is it important? What is the life lesson you need to learn?
- What will force you to change (or refuse to change)?
- What must you sacrifice?
- What final scene or image will prove the change?

Task 16
Who Is Your Reader?

> 'We read to know we are not alone.'
> **William Nicholson**

HOME IN. REMEMBER, REAL PEOPLE read books. They are chosen and bought by individuals who stay up late at night reading your words.

Why will someone want to read your book? Who are they? What are they looking for? What will they find?

On the most basic level:

- ✓ Readers of a non-fiction are looking for information.
- ✓ Readers of a memoir are looking for information, or connection.
- ✓ Readers of a novel are looking to be entertained.

So as you offer your story up you need to ask yourself, as author, who cares what I have to say?

Offer your reader an interesting premise (or argument) and serve up an entertaining story, and you will have solved the 'who cares' question. But the 'who cares' question also calls on you to find something bigger than your story.

If you are writing a straightforward non-fiction book about sales techniques, the 'who cares' is clear. Sales staff who want to increase their figures care!

But how do you make someone care if you are writing a memoir or biography? How do you touch something in THEM?

This happens if you realize that your book is not really about YOU. It's not. It's about something bigger than you. Most often when you read a memoir or non-fiction you are not that interested in the person who wrote it. You are interested in what *happened* and how they handled it, right? I don't know you, but I may know your *story* because it has happened to me. Or someone close to me. Or I fear that it will happen to me.

Likewise, we are not reading your story because of what happened to you (or your subject). We are reading your story because it is about something in our lives. And that thing is a universal thing.

Remember, you do not need everybody to read your book. That is impossible. You are only looking for readers who will resonate with your story, your style or your particular voice. Your story does not have to be a new one. Or a remarkable one. In fact, most stories have been told again and again and again. Your story has been told before. But your task as a writer is to simply tell your version in your unique way, to a new audience.

How will somebody recognize themselves in your story?

Whose life do you want to change?

What problems do you want to solve?

Your job going forward is to take the focus off YOU and think about what your reader wants to find in your book.

Ask yourself:

- ✓ How does this relate to your Big Idea?
- ✓ Can you make your Big Idea tighter now so it more directly draws a reader in?

WRITING TASK

Answer the questions below:

- Who is going to buy and read your book?
- Where do they live?
- What is their gender?
- What language do they speak?
- What is their age?
- What are their jobs or careers?
- What are their interests?
- Why will they read your book?
- Who should not read your book?

Once you have these answers, write them as a blurb that can be included in your proposal. It should look a bit like this:

This book is for senior managers, CFOs and anyone who wants to get ahead in their game.

Write a series of questions

Write questions that speak directly to your reader. Use the word 'you'.

This list will form part of your book proposal. It will speak to why readers will be reading your book.

Format

Fill in the sentences below as if you are talking directly to a reader. Aim for a few sentences in each one.

- Have you ever worried about/thought about …?
- Have you ever wondered/desired/questioned …?

This book is for you.

- You with ...
- You are going to find out ...
- It will tell you my story/the story of ...
- It will show you ...
- It will leave you feeling ...

For example:
Do you want to clear your debt? Do you find that you always run out of money early in the month? Do you ever save? Do you have any financial back-up plans?

HEART EXERCISE

You should be writing steadily by now. By this we mean getting stuck into the actual scenes and chapters. Are you? Have you even started? Or are you still thinking about it, with no actual words on the page? Every writer has their own writing discipline and style—some start with bursts of creative writing and excited writing immersion, followed by quieter, non-writing periods. Or you might start off strong and then keep writing steadily for the entire duration, your word count climbing week by week. Or perhaps you are the kind of writer who does a lot of planning upfront, starts off slowly but finds your real rhythm later on as you charge to the finish line. Perhaps you are still figuring out your style and finding your groove?

The sooner you know your favorite and most inspired writing time, pace and style, the easier it is to block off writing times that fit in with your preferred writing style.

But you do need to be writing. Take five minutes to sit quietly and figure out where you are right now.

Be honest with yourself about what is working with your writing discipline and what isn't? Is there a small tweak you can make to increase your word count?

TASK 17

Do Some Research

> 'Read a thousand books, and your words will flow like a river.'
>
> **Lisa See**

NAIL DOWN YOUR STRUCTURE THIS week by doing some competitive research. Pop into a real bookshop (not an online one) and spend some time there. Go to 'your shelf'—that shelf on which your book is going to sit. Look at all books that are similar to the one you are writing.

These books are the competitive titles in the GENRE you have chosen. Note them down because you will use them later when you write your proposal. It is critical to know your competition. Remember, we are not suggesting you buy these books and devour every word written. In fact, remember not to read the book (take another look at Sarah's rules in Task 11). Your task here is to look at the technical make-up of your competitors' books for research.

Get a sense of the following:

- ✓ Look at how the book is structured—is it in themes, chronological, or according to ideas? How did they do this and does it work?
- ✓ Check out 'the way' they write.
- ✓ Notice the TONE of voice they use when they write. (Is it chatty/humorous/all business/big sisterly?)

- ✓ Do they keep it personal or is it strictly business?
- ✓ Do they talk directly to the reader by using 'you', or do they use the third person 'they'?
- ✓ How long are the chapters?
- ✓ Do they have sections and subsections?
- ✓ Do they use text boxes or any other features?
- ✓ What elements do they have in common?

Note down the name of the publisher (you can possibly submit your book to them further down the line).

You will use some of the titles of these books later when you write your synopsis.

WRITING TASK

Create a series of one-liners to describe what other books your book is similar to.

For example:

- It is a fable-based parable, much like *The Celestine Prophecy* by James Redfield.
- It is a business success book in the vein of *2.5 Unstoppable Laws of Selling* by Jeffrey Gitomer.
- It's a hilarious account of travels through India, much like *Air Babylon* by Imogen Edwards-Jones.
- It's a personal, heart-centered story about the loss of my child, much like *Get Me to 21* by Gabi Lowe.
- It's an inspirational sport memoir about my fight back from serious injury, in the vein of *It's Not About the Bike* by Lance Armstrong.

BAM! In one line we (and you) know what your book will be like.

Are you using your Weekly Word Tracker?

The way our serious writers always reach their goals is pre-empting each week what they are going to commit to. Then every Monday checking in with their progress and reporting back on how they did in the week gone by on our FB group. You can also just check in with yourself, with a writing buddy or a writing group. How seriously are you taking this?

The more specific and in-your-face you can be, the better.

YOUR WORD COUNT TARGET IS 15,000 WORDS

TASK 18

Who Else Is In Your Book?

> 'Her lips full and inviting, she has an infectious laugh and glassy cackle in her eyes, and a 2000 volt sexual charisma that beckons me like a fluff girl on scuffed knees.'
>
> **Brett Tate**

EVEN THOUGH YOU MAY BE the main character, this book is not just about you. Even non-fiction needs other characters. And many of them. You can't stand alone so you are going to need a cast of characters to fill the pages, and to fill the world you are building on paper. Giving yourself friends, family and a past is what makes your story come alive.

Who else should have some airtime in your book? How will you write them in?

Some will pop in and leave, others will stay the course of the book.

- ✓ Who are they?
- ✓ Where do they fit in?
- ✓ Do you talk to them in the book?
- ✓ How do they weave into your story?
- ✓ Should they have some scenes without you in them?
- ✓ Will they be able to tell their own story in their own voice?
- ✓ Might you tell their story in a text box? (For example, a client's story.)

- ✓ May they talk about you?
- ✓ Will they challenge or support you?

These are some of the people you may want to include in your story.

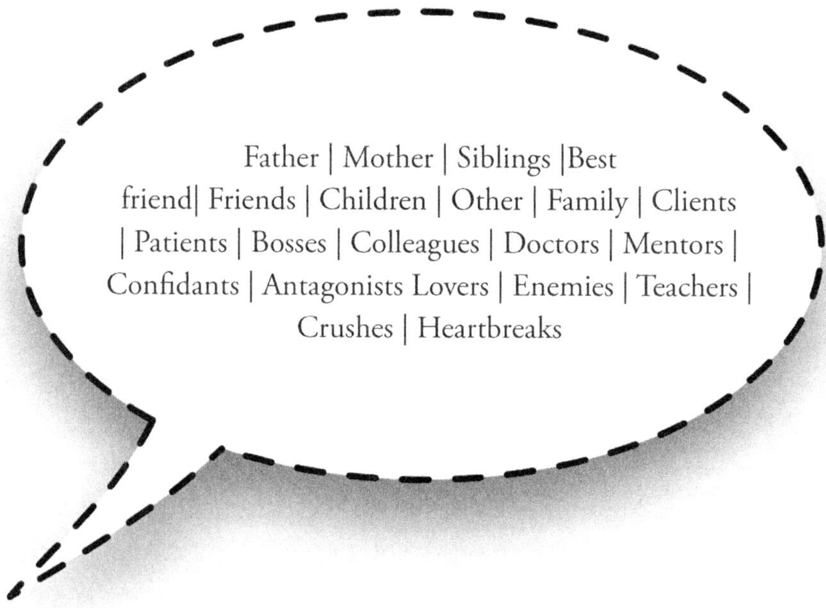

If you are writing a memoir, it is a great idea to make a page that represents each decade of your story. List the people who were important in your life in that decade.

- ✓ Start with the obvious and expand it.
- ✓ Add names, details and dates.
- ✓ Who is a small character you can leave out and which small characters are important?
- ✓ Which small characters can you add for color and detail?
- ✓ Who can you leave out because they don't really move your story forward?
- ✓ Do you have an eccentric person who can add color?

Tips on writing about others

- ✓ Work on developing a cast of eight other key people in your book
- ✓ Make sure one of them is consistent, a person who is there for the entire journey with you. They don't need to be at your side, but need to simply be there. Lance Armstrong uses his mother. Who is your 'constant'?
- ✓ Keep your cast small. If you have a family of 10, focus on two of them. If you have hundreds of clients, rather share just a few of the most relevant stories
- ✓ Describe them clearly and carefully the very first time we meet each of them
- ✓ Make them come alive as real characters
- ✓ Only chose big-impact people to name and develop fully
- ✓ Let them talk to you and to each other
- ✓ Roll them naturally into your story
- ✓ If you are not going to develop them, don't name them and don't describe them. Rather give them generic titles like 'the neighbor', 'a client', and 'the doctor'.

WRITING TASK

Make a long list today of the people you have forgotten to include in your book. How you are now going in include them?

Write a scene today in which one of them is talking to you (or talking about you).

HEART EXERCISE

Find your book an anchor. This is an exquisite, inspirational item you can keep on your desk to keep you inspired, focused and anchored in your writing process.

Some ideas could include plants, flowers, photographs, inspirational quotes, crystals, a special water jug and glass, and so on. Be creative and find something meaningful for YOU and this book you are writing.

When I wrote my second book, *Ditch Your Glitch*, as you already know, I was on a very tight two-month deadline, so I needed to stay uber focused. There was no time or space to muck about. I was also facilitating a Mastermind process for 11 clients, other writers who had committed to tackling a similar deadline with me. PRESSURE! It was also the starting point of how Sarah and I started working together, so that time remains forever etched in my heart as a pivotal point in my business.

Being the one who embodies my LIVE LIGHT LIVE LARGE motto, of course I had already created the most amazing writing nook and space in my treehouse (you did that for yourself back in my suggestions in the 'set up strong' section, right?). But I also needed something very specific for THIS project. I went on a little hunt, and finally found myself a beautiful muse—a small yet magnificent potted Ficus plant—and she magnificently held the energy of my book for me on my desk. I needed what I refer to as an 'anchor' or a muse. I put a picture of her on my Facebook page and asked my tribe what they thought the plant's name should be … and someone up came the suggestion of Bianca. It was an instant Yes! Only then did I make the connection that this plant was my living reminder to BE ANCHORED! Got it?

TASK 19

Make Yourself More Physical

> 'Her skin glistening in the neon light coming from the paved court through the slits in the blind, her soot-black lashes matted, her grave gray eyes more vacant than ever.'
>
> ***Lolita*, Vladimir Nabokov**

OFTEN AS WRITERS WE SHY away from the physical actions of our characters and stick to what they are thinking or feeling. But readers want more! They want to live in your skin, walk in your shoes, eat with your family and live your life for a few hundred pages.

How do you write like this? You get more physical and you embody your character by using words.

Trick 1: Characters all alone should do more than think

While you are thinking and plotting and planning, don't become disembodied. You need to pace, act, move, smell, taste, plan and inhabit the space. Keep linking your thoughts back to your body. The reader not only wants to know what you look like, they want to know what your physical body feels like and how it moves. They want to actually live in someone else's body for a while. For this book, it's yours. This means you need to let a reader know what it likes to feel to be you.

This is how Costa Carastavrakis did it in *I am Costa, From Meth to Marathons.*

> *It's a Sunday night. My mouth has a metallic taste that comes with permanent thirst; stale with a dry yet sticky feel on my tongue. My face and neck muscles are tired and stiff from contracting and contorting my features endlessly.*
>
> *That's what my face does on crystal meth.*
>
> *My eyes open extra wide and my jaw wider. Then I pull a huge smile to stretch my face. That's stage one. Then I use my face muscles to pinch my face at the mouth and nose.*
>
> *Stretch. Pull. Hold the ridiculous face. Relax. Repeat. Repeat. Repeat. Endlessly.*
>
> *I pull a long deep breath and for a moment, I can feel my heartbeat.*
>
> *Then I am in freefall.*
>
> *That's what it feels like.*
>
> *I've been pushed off a building and I can't stop falling.*
>
> *Hang on ... now it feels like I'm floating. Not falling any more.*
>
> *My eyes droop and jaw relaxes.*
>
> *I'm hit by a wave of warmth and my shoulders drop.*
>
> *I tense up and frown a stern face. Then the cycle starts again —contracting and contorting my features.*
>
> *Then I'm falling again.*
>
> *Or is this the first time?*
>
> ***I am Costa, From Meth to Marathons,***
> Costa Carastavrakis

Trick 2: You reveal yourself (and others) in setting

Be wary of disembodied characters. Real people are always SOMEWHERE. Where are you? Don't over-explain and over-describe every location. Rather simply place your characters in their setting. Where is this conversation taking place? Not in the ether … make sure it's in the real world.

> *Having spent the better part of ten years working for this airline, you'd have thought I'd have a better parking spot by now. Somewhere within the airport at least where I could park up in the short-stay multi-storey and walk across without getting bloody rained on. But no. As duty manager I'm one of the most senior employees my airline has working over here in the UK; I'm in charge of all that goes on in the airport and I am still parking my car at the bloody north perimeter fence along with all the other riff-raff.*
>
> ***Air Babylon, A Mile-High Journey through the Best-Kept Secrets of the Airline Industry,***
> Imogen Edwards-Jones & Anonymous

Trick 3: You highlight your quirks and flaws

As an author, you will choose what elements of yourself you want to share with the reader. You don't have to reveal everything. But give them some juicy things to relate to. Share a habit, an obsession, and a past. Give your readers a part of your personality they will never forget. Do you collect something? Covet something? Obsess about something? Have a hobby? Do you have a hidden trauma, a fabulous skill or a deadly secret? Are you bloody minded, or temperamental, or a terrible cook? Or better yet, all three. Do you have a quirk or a way of seeing the world that is unique? Share that.

Flaws make characters more interesting, especially if the character has to face their flaws.

- James Frey is a lying, cowering, charming, and drug-addled addict in *A Million Little Pieces.*
- Deepak Chopra is a Zen, enlightened pioneer in mind-body medicine in *Syncro Destiny.*
- Lance Armstrong is an arrogant, impossibly competitive athlete with a self-confessed God Complex in *It's Not About the Bike.*

How can you characterize yourself (and others) as succinctly as you may craft a lead character in a novel?

WRITING TASK

Write a scene in which you reveal your own worst possible behavior very clearly to your reader. No excuses. Just describe what you do and how you do it in a moment of rage, jealousy or fear.

Here's what Sharon Osborne does in her autobiography *Extreme!* when she finds out her father was having an affair and she finds the lady's pink knickers.

So I went upstairs to the tower room, picked up this stone gorilla and lugged it down to the front door. It was about two feet high and made of concrete. On the head of the monkey I arranged the pink knickers. And then I lifted up my skirt, squatted down and shat on it. So there was the fucking gorilla, vaguely Buddha-like, pink knickers on its head, topped with a turd.

TASK 20

Get Talking

> 'I'm the Anti-Christ. You got me in a vendetta kind of mood. You tell the angels in heaven you never seen evil so singularly personified as you did in the face of the man who killed you. My name is Vincent Coccotti.'
>
> **Vincent Coccotti, *True Romance***

DIALOGUE MAKES A STORY, AND your characters, come alive. It moves you away from thinking and telling. Remember that we challenged you to make sure you have other people in your story. This is why. Modern books include a lot of dialogue.

Your comfort zone as a writer is to write interior monologue or narration. That means you are caught in the zone of a character thinking, thinking, thinking. But you need to talk continually in a book. Allow your words to reveal your personality.

See how Lance Armstrong uses a lot of dialogue between himself and doctors in his memoir *It's Not About the Bike.*

> *Once a doctor has cracked open your skull and put you back together there is a moment of truth. No matter how good the surgeon is he waits anxiously to see if everything moves and whether the patient is properly responsive.*
>
> *'Do you remember me,' he said.*

'You're my doctor,' I said.

'What's my name?'

'Scott Shapiro.'

'Can you tell me your name?'

'Lance Armstrong,' I said. 'And I can kick your ass on a bike any day.'

Are you (as the lead character) actually talking or just thinking?

Is your entire piece an entire interior monologue with a smattering of dialogue?

Are you allowing other characters into your story? Are they talking?

Who are the characters who now need to start talking? Your dad, mom, sister, clients, boss, doctors, psychologist?

You now need to push yourself to shift into dialogue as you move forward in your writing.

I want to know what you said to your dad when you visited him at the psych ward. What did he say to you? How did he go mad? What crazy stuff did he say? What did friends, family, doctors, psychologists say?

This is the difference of **showing** versus **telling**. You are TELLING us he went mad. Show us with his words, no words, rambling, screaming. Lance Armstrong doesn't tell us he is alert and sharp after having his brain tumour removed, he shows us.

Extract from *The Glass Castle* by Jeanette Wallis

'I think that maybe sometimes people get the lives they want.'

'Are you saying homeless people want to live on the streets?' Professor Fuchs asked. 'Are you saying they don't want warm beds and roofs over their heads?'

'Not exactly,' I said. I was fumbling for words. 'They do. But if some of them were willing to work hard and make compromises, they might not have ideal lives, but they could make ends meet.'

Professor Fuchs walked around from behind her lectern. 'What do you know about the lives of the underprivileged?' she asked. She was practically trembling with agitation. 'What do you know about the hardships and obstacles that the underclass face?'

How will other people talk in your book?

- ✓ They can talk to you, or about you
- ✓ You can use design such as, 'My Story' boxes to allow others to talk or share their story. This is ideal for non-fiction
- ✓ You can give them a monologue: a long speech by one character to you.
- ✓ You can include an email or note that another person sent you that allows them to present their side of the case.

Remember to include the interior thoughts of your viewpoint character (you) as you talk. You cannot present what another person is thinking—only you.

WRITING TASK

Today you will write a scene that is dialogue driven. Up to 70% of the information in the scene needs to be delivered in the form of a conversation between two people. No small talk is allowed. Only conversations that drive the plot forward or present conflict are allowed in books.

- What are they talking about?
- Who is in the conversation?
- Why are they arguing?

HEART EXERCISE

Time to be honest now—what's your self-talk like at the moment? What is that inner critic voice that sits inside your head telling you (or yelling at you)?

Are you being kind and nudging yourself forward with encouragement and positive re-enforcement? Telling yourself you can absolutely do this even if it's the first time you are writing a book? Or are you being a little too negative and harsh about your ill-perceived writing abilities? Or is your critic running rampant and berating every sentence you're writing or your procrastination thereof?

Which voice is louder at the moment?

As a writer, one of the biggest challenges to completing your first draft, is not so much the lack of technical skill, but more the mental beliefs you hold around your writing ability. And possibly a lack of writing discipline.

What practical action can you take today to ease up on yourself and get the right heartfelt support? If you are on our private Facebook group, maybe you could come and share your writing fears, your inner critic and be a little more vulnerable? I guarantee you will be so surprised how much support you experience when you share in our trusted space. Or reach out to someone you trust, respect and admire (friend, colleague, mentor or therapist to move you gently through any negative doldrums.)

KEY TIP

We honestly don't want you to be simply reading this book – it's a workbook.

We want you to be writing and increasing your word count, day by day, week by week towards your 50,000 word count goal. And bravely slaying any dragons en route that are trying to stop you from reaching your goal.

TASK 21

The Types of Scenes You Need

> 'I am 54 years old. Large important parts of my life receive virtually no attention in my memoir—a sentence for a traumatic love affair, a page for four happy years in college. Memoirs are selections from your life story, shaped by theme, driven by a few burning questions. So the question the reader brings is: why these bits of your life?'
>
> **Kevin Fenton, *Leaving Rollingstone***

IF YOU ARE FOLLOWING THE rules here you are moving forward by filling in your chapters (NF) or you are working through your scene list (M). Let's now look at how you can vary your writing style by including different kinds of elements or scenes.

Here are a few ways you may want to mix up your writing and your story. These are chapters or scenes you may need in your book

You need chapters or scenes that 'set the scene'

These are overview scenes. You may want a scene that covers an entire lifetime. You may want to write this in the style of a narrator or journalist.

For example:

- What is Taoism?
- Why sales is the master game
- Why health matters
- Carbs are your enemy – here's why
- What is mindfulness about?
- The rock scene in London in the '80s.

You need chapters or scenes that are technical

All books need a deep dive into the nitty-gritty. If you are covering a specialized topic you may need to really research and unpack this for your reader. This may also be your personal expertise that you need to convey with authority to the reader. In a memoir you may want to play some of these out as conversations.

For example:

- How motor neuron disease affects the nerves? (Could this be a doctor explaining it to you?)
- How the body processes carbs
- How the Wall Street crash unfolded
- The ins and outs of property law.

You need chapters or scenes to compress time

Some chapters require that you sometimes sum up years, even decades of your life or experience, into a single sentence, page or chapter.

Which times in your life do you need to do this?
How can you skip longer sections?
How can you move from action to action?

You need chapters or scenes that are exciting and speed things up

Some scenes require pace and excitement. Short words. Short sentences. Tight dialogue. This can express anger. Excitement. Fear. Urgency. Clipped tone. One-liners. Fast pace.

Can you find a sense of urgency? Can you make it shorter, tighter, more exciting, closer?

You need chapters or scenes that slow down the time

Your book absolutely must have some key BIG moments that need to play out ever so slowly over a full scene and evoke every sense. Often these big moments play out over one to two chapters even. As a writer you need to find out these bigger moments in your story and draw things out. Describe every sensory detail. Hold the reader in THAT moment of time. Make them feel it all.

You need chapters or scenes in the present tense

Using present tense can add a different tone to your writing. Please note the entire book cannot be in present tense as this is jarring to the reader. Stick to using it for impact in select scenes where it is very real and immediate.

> Here's an example:
> *She looks at me. I look at her. We know it is real. We are about to get mugged.*
>
> *I run to the door. It's closed. I open it quickly and race outside, heart jacking in my chest like a drum.*

WRITING TASK

Write a scene or a chapter that is a slow and languid 'moment that lasts forever' in your life. It can be in the present tense or simple past tense.

In your upcoming writing days you are going to include all of the above styles in scenes or chapters to start adding color and variety to your writing.

YOUR WORD COUNT TARGET IS 25,000

TASK 22
Can We Hear Your Voice?

'How wild it was, to let it be.'
Cheryl Strayed, *Wild*

HOW DO YOU FIND YOUR true voice when you write? Writers so often ask me this. They say, Sarah, it is hard to find what sort of voice I genuinely feel is me when I write.

Often our brains are so full of all the authors we have read, all the poems and stories. They are full of what 'good' writing is so it is hard to discover your own style beyond all these other voices.

I think of your writing voice as a song that you have to discover by removing all the other voices. The song is ancient. But how do you find YOURS?

Many tribal people believe that every person has a particular song that connects them to other realms. In Africa, many believe that each song has a very particular beat on the drum and that it calls you to dance. We believe that when the song and the drum and the dance are in harmony, they connect you to your soul, your ancestors, God or spirit.

All of these songs carry forward all the stories and all the pain and love of the world. The song is what connects you to this timeless wave—it brings forward all the stories of love and loss, of heroes and adventures.

It is a song that comes from the older world and time long ago when rhythms were set at night under the stars, and where bare feet beat out the ageless dances. Have you ever heard songs that evoke some ancient memory? They may be Irish or Greek or Indian—but they speak to you of old memories and love.

Now all of these songs are good ones. But how do you find YOUR particular song?

In writing, this song is not made of a melody, but of the words we choose to tell our story.

It is the particularly unique quality, tone and timbre we bring to a story. It is where you chose to be intelligent, funny, soulful, brash, clear, fast or magical in the words you bring to the page.

You bring all of who you are to your writing.

First you have to write in all the voices you think you should use to write. You will try to be intelligent, sardonic, profound, funny, academic and provocative. You will tell a story you think others will love. You mimic other writers and other stories. This is the process of learning.

When I first started writing, I desperately wanted to sound like a magic realist and I was obsessed with Gabriel García Márquez and Isabel Allende.They have magical words that weave a story of poetry and song.

What came out was totally different. It was modern, funny and ... sort of simple and real really.

This is what I have found true of most writers. If you keep going and just write, all the ideas and other voices may drop away. And what will be left is your real voice.

Most often it will be far simpler, cleaner and less complicated than you expected. Less clever. More real. More readable. Our real voices often come out when we write about what we care about, or something we have an emotional stake in.

The journey of writing will lead you to find your true writing voice. You cannot find it by thinking about it, or by asking your old English teacher, or mimicking sassy magazine copy. No, you find it by just writing.

Day after day. Just keep on writing. Slowly all the constructs of language will drop away onto the pages and what you will be left with is your writing voice. Your song.

BUT also remember that in non-fiction you also do need a tone that is ENGAGING and EXCITING.

One of the great pleasures of writing is also that you can create a distinct voice and personality for your book. And for your literary self. This can be a conscious choice and does not have to reflect your speaking voice or real personality. Tone or voice means the writing style or attitude you are going to use. The voice or tone in a memoir is extremely important in getting a reader's attention and in bringing the audience into the story emotionally. Tone helps to give you a distinct personality your reader can grasp onto, follow and like.

List of tones

Funny | Badass | Serious |
Heartfelt | Irreverent | Angry | Ominous |
Gentle | Nurturing | Sassy | Hilarious | Vengeful |
Provocative | Chatty | Academic | Challenging | Direct |
Businesslike | Professional | Big sisterly | Inspirational | Informal |
Bossy | Confessional | Simple | Sarcastic | Respectful | Devotional
| Empathetic | Kickass | Nostalgic | Regretful | Authoritative |
Desperate | Clear | Epic | Argumentative

There are many ways you can write the same book or convey the same idea.

You may find up to now you have just been writing in 'your voice'.

- ✓ Is there a better tone to tell this story in?
- ✓ Have you considered a tone that is more entertaining?
- ✓ Can you find words that create this on the page?

WRITING TASK

What tone or voice are you going to use to write your book?

Sarah says

For my first book I settled on the tone 'sassy bitch' (I was known for being a humor writer, don't judge), and the second was 'big sister' (warm and wise, a bit like Oprah).

Kate says

My first book was 'kickass', my second was 'compassion with a kick', and my third 'respectful yet bossy'.

This week you are going to write two of your planned scenes, but in each, you will use totally different tones for each scene. I am going to recommend the tones below, but you can also choose ones more fitting to the genre you are going to write.

So you will write **ONE using HUMOR** and the **SECOND using a CONFESSIONAL** tone.

Humor does not mean you need to crack a joke. It means you need to see the funny side of your situation or story. It means you tell it with lightness and a laugh.

Confessional means you share deeply of yourself; you tell all the details without holding anything back.

HEART EXERCISE

You are going to find a tone mentor. Who is the one person—living or dead—whom you would love to impress with your book? Who embodies your tone?

Oprah? Khalil Gibran? Amy Schumer? Brene Brown? Tony Robbins?

Now find a picture of your tone mentor and stick it above your writing desk or paste it in your notebook if you are a café writer. When you lose your way with your tone, take a look at them. What would make your tone mentor proud?

Sarah says

For my first book (sassy bitch), my tone mentor was Madonna. She was super-hot in the year 2005. She was kickass, straight talking, no BS and super controversial. I had a killer picture of her in a tux bottoms and no top, showing her breasts, with her ripped arms, chewing a cigar and taking on the world. When my book bored me, I knew she would be bored too by my writing. I knew it was not good enough, so it challenged me to really find a fun, engaging, but authentic voice.

TASK 23
Who's Causing Trouble in Your Story?

> 'Why aren't crazy people content to take over, like, one town? It always has to be the whole word.'
> **James Patterson, *Angel***

WHAT! YOU ASK. WHY TROUBLE? Why would I need anyone to do this in a book?

Have you ever heard that books are driven by conflict? This word conflict means that all books are driven by things that go wrong, not things that go right. If everything went your way it wouldn't be a very exciting story, would it?

One key way of creating conflict is to use a character who challenges you. In fact, all of the characters in a memoir should challenge you.

All books need a character like this in some shape or form.

In a novel, these antagonists are cut and dried and form the basis of all plotting.

But how does this work when you are writing about yourself, an idea, or your expertise? What if there wasn't anyone obvious who caused trouble or challenged you?

You are not writing a novel, but you still need to find them. But from within your own life.

Most antagonists from your life are not cut-and-dried baddies or evil people, but simply people who challenge you, the status quo, or your ideals or journey. Sometimes you do have a clear and obvious villain. like the kidnapper, an abusive father, compulsive liar, cheating wife, gambling and coke-snorting ex or your corrupt business partner.

But most autobiographic writers do not have villains to portray, just plain disagreeable people. Disagreements, miscommunication, moral muddles, wrong-headedness and incompatible goals provide enough conflict without needing an outright baddie.

Most often the people who challenge you are just regular people. And often they are family.

Kate says

In my second book, *Ditch Your Glitch*, a recurring character was my father, who continually challenged my choices and path.

Sarah says

In my second book, *Can Your Relationship Survive Your Children (And Other Passion Killers)*, the antagonists were the rug rats themselves.

So who are the characters (or clients) in your book who can create a level of conflict?

- ✓ They are known as the villain or antagonist, but may not be evil at all
- ✓ They must be a person, ideally a whole load of them
- ✓ They cannot be an idea, the weather, a company, or your own alter ego or personal demons
- ✓ They have goals in direct conflict with your own
- ✓ They must be able to fight a good fight against you
- ✓ They challenge you (and perhaps make you stronger, better, or clearer about your own path).

How to write about these people

- ✓ **Reveal them through their own actions, not your judgements.** There is no real need to call them names. Readers can make their own judgements; that is how they participate in the writing
- ✓ **Let them talk for themselves.** Use dialogue for this. Dialogue allows characters to reveal themselves, in their own words.
- ✓ **Use telling details.** If you call a client pretentious and uptight, it's an open-and-shut case, but if you give details about him and how he handles his staff, the readers can come to that conclusion themselves
- ✓ **Show them as a person.** If you have no compassion or psychological insight, it will show and then a reader won't like you. If you include all sides of a person, the dark and the light, then it is possible to tell even ugly truths about someone without committing character assassination.

WRITING TASK

Focus on one particularly challenging character you want to include in your book. If you don't have one, it's time to write one into your book.

Fill this in to make them come alive (for you and the reader):

- ✎ Favorite words:
- ✎ Sayings:
- ✎ Motto:
- ✎ Always gives this advice:
- ✎ Best swear words:
- ✎ Nicknames for you:

- Nicknames for them:
- Excited mode:
- Angry mode:
- Joke style:
- Dress sense:
- Physical quirks:

Now write a scene that includes your character. Remember that as we first meet any character, you need to describe them physically (that means what they look like). Then write a scene in which you let them tell you why THEY are right, and YOU are wrong.

Use mostly dialogue in this scene.

Make sure to include your interior thoughts as they are speaking to you.

HEART EXERCISE

Grab your journal and spend a little moment checking in with yourself. Answer these questions:

- What is currently WORKING about my book: the story and the people in it?
- What is NOT WORKING about my book?
- How can I tackle my next few writing days differently to catapult forward?
- If my ideal reader read my book right now, as it is, they would say ...

Task 24
Are You Talking To Your Reader?

> 'When I sit down to write a book, I do not say to myself, "I am going to produce a work of art." I write it because there is some lie that I want to expose, some fact to which I want to draw attention, and my initial concern is to get a hearing.'
>
> **George Orwell**

TODAY, TAKE A LOOK AT the actual words you have used in your writing so far.

Ask yourself:

- ✓ Are talking to your reader at all?
- ✓ Are you ignoring them completely?

There are a number of ways you can talk to your reader to engage them more. Most often you can use all of these techniques to differing effect.

You can use the word 'you', where you talk to them directly.

For example:

'Breakthroughs start when you start thinking about a problem in a fresh new way.' *Synchro Destiny,* Deepak Chopra

or

Have you ever found yourself wondering ...?

Are you willing to change ...?
Do you have what it takes to follow this program?
Do you want to be a better boss?

You can use the word 'us' and 'we' when you talk as if you are one of them.

For example:
'As children we loved our bodies and rarely thought about them ...'
Synchro Destiny, Deepak Chopra
or
So there is one thing holding us back as parents ...
Aren't we all taught at school that ...?
When we want to de-clutter our homes, it's important to ...

You may not talk to them at all, and rather use the neutral voice of a reporter or 'reportage'.

For example:
'The brain's vestibular system is very complex ...' *Synchro Destiny,* Deepak Chopra
or
Are people willing to change?
There are four reasons a negotiation can fall through.

You can mix up all of the three styles in the same book by using different voices in different scenes as shown by Deepak Chopra.

Remember:
- ✓ Stick to one key voice or way of addressing readers as your overall book tone
- ✓ Some scenes can use other voices.

When you start becoming more aware of how you talk to your reader, a few things might converge. The overall tone you have already chosen to tell this particular story will also determine how you address your reader.

How you speak to them also sets up the result or outcome you want readers to reach by the end of the book. For NF your particular form of expertise will also influence your choice of tone and how you talk to your reader.

WRITING TASK

Spend some time deciding which of these styles suits you and your book best.

Can you stretch yourself to get more interactive and more engaging with your reader as you write going forward? What might you do differently in writing the next scene?

Write a key scene today in which you talk directly to your reader and explain to them what is going on for you.

HEART EXERCISE

It is time to do a word count reality check-in.

If you are being pretty consistent in how often you do the tasks, you are probably tacking one blast of writing every couple of days. So now, at Task 24, you should be over halfway, sitting close to 35,000 words on your manuscript.

Yikes—how are you doing?

Does this check-in make your heart palpitate with anxiety or sing with pride?

Please don't let this check-in stop you in your tracks. It's about accountability and following your dream. Your dream of writing, remember? If it helps, go back to your very first exercise about WHY you wanted to write this book, and why you were so willing to commit. Because this is where it really matters. Dig deeper, writer, dig deeper!

You might have to sit down now, look at your diary, reorganize your schedule and up the ante. If you go back to the SET UP STRONG section, I suggested you block off writing time (bum time) as well as longer retreat-type immersions. Let's get that on the radar and booked. How soon can you grab a few days to yourself to really push your word count up? Don't let yourself get too distracted with all the tasks we give you—your first draft is about completing it in the 100 days from when you started. We wouldn't have given this book the title it has, if we didn't absolutely know it was possible.

So—take a big, deep breath and keep going. Well done for getting this far! You are way further along than you probably think you are. You are further along than other people who 'want to write a book'. You are doing it.

YOUR WORD COUNT TARGET IS 35,000 WORDS

Task 25

Tell The Truth (With Courage and Compassion)

> 'Other people's memories of the stuff in this book might not be the same as mine. I ain't gonna argue with 'em. Over the past forty years I've been loaded on booze, coke, acid, Quaalude, glue, cough mixture, heroin, Rohypnol, Klonopin, Vicodin, and too many other heavy-duty substances to list in this footnote. On more than a few occasions I was on all of those at the same time. I'm not the fucking *Encyclopedia Britannica*, put it that way. What you read here is what dribbled out of the jelly I call my brain when I asked it for my life story. Nothing more, nothing less.'
>
> ***Ozzy*, Ozzy Osborne**

THE ASSUMPTION IN ALL NON-FICTION books is that they are fact-based and driven by truth. This seems straightforward in a NF.

- ✓ How does this work in a memoir?
- ✓ How do you know it is the truth?
- ✓ And whose version of the truth is this?
- ✓ Are there other versions?

There is only one way to tell the truth when you write, and that is to 'write what you know'. That means you are recording your story as clearly as you can remember it.

Do you remember what your father said to you when you were 12? No. So most of the time you are going to have to recreate scenes and dialogue. Do your best to use the intention of the person—even though we know you can't remember the actual words any more. You HAVE to make them up. That is assumed in biographical writing and it totally fine.

The more notes you have, records, diaries, emails and text messages that contain the 'truth' the better. Use these in your writing.

WRITING TASK

Write the disclaimer that will sit at the front of your book. This is a short piece in which you forgive yourself for the faults of memory and explain to the reader why you are writing this book.

Here's how Norman Mailer's wife Norris Church Mailer did it in *A Ticket to the Circus, A Memoir.*

Everything in this book is true. At least, it's true for me. Memory is treacherous, and we probably have all said, 'glad to meet you' to people we have met before. Sometimes we have had whole conversations—or even more than that—with them and still don't' remember them, which gets complicated and embarrassing. (Once my husband argued with a woman who claimed they had dated that she was mistaken. And then on the cab ride home he slapped his forehead and said, 'She's right!') But to the best of my knowledge, all the things I've written about in this book happened to me. There are instances where I have changed the names of people and I have said, 'Let's call her ...' I have used first names for the most part, although at times I have used whole names. No real reason. I just thought some people might like not to be totally identified. A few times, no name has been used at all. These stories are probably not the good ones.

It's funny, the things that mean so much to one person and nothing to another, and the small thoughtless comment that inadvertently cuts to the quick. I didn't intend to hurt anyone in the telling of my story, and if I did, I apologies now before you read it. Please know I went into this with a good heart, and I hope that comes through.

A Ticket to the Circus, Norris Church Mailer

Think about this …

- What are you 'not entirely sure are true' in your story?
- Who may tell another version?
- Who might take offense to what you are sharing in this book?
- Should you ask permission?
- Is there anyone who may be hurt?
- Are there any legal ramifications like defamation or libel you need to consider?
- Does your family need to know what you are about to reveal?

kate says

It was a very considered decision not to pre-share any of the contents of my second book, *Ditch Your Glitch*, with my family. It had a memoir aspect woven in though the book to add insight to the coaching exercises I was asking readers to work through, highlighting why each exercise was important. I checked in with my publisher as to whether they felt I should share it with my family, and they responded that there was nothing that needed permission or sign-off by them, as it was simply my personal story woven into a non-fiction 'how-to' coaching book. Therefore, no legal libel, just simply my decision. It was dedicated to both my parents, but my dad had already passed on, so my mum was very touched and quite emotional when I read her the dedication live on video, as she was in the UK and I was in South Africa when I received my first copies.

Only a few months later, when we were gallivanting in the USA for my movie premiere in Las Vegas, did I get to put a copy in her paws as we retired to bed that first night. Lo and behold, the next morning when I knocked on her door and gave her a cup of tea, she was in tears. She was wide-eyed and sobbing, saying she had never known all that time I had been bulimic and how could she not have known. It led to interesting conversations and of course I had to ask myself the question: should I have told my family before, or given them a draft copy as a heads-up before it was published?

You have to make that decision for yourself, and be clear about the one you make. For me, it was never my intention to hurt her, and maybe I could have done it differently, but it was still the right way for me to release the book. Be clear in your heart about every decision you make!

Sarah says

Ah, the truth. It is not always pretty. I was pretty clear after writing my first book that my husband was okay with it. Most of my style is poking fun at myself rather than others. But still I gave him the manuscript before I sent it off. He read a few pages, yawned and looked up.

'This is not really my kind of read. It's a book for women. Do I really have to read the whole thing?'

I raised an eyebrow.

'Is there anything in this I need to know about that could be alarming? Or illegal? For either of us?' he asked.

He had been subject to years of my writing in women's magazines and sharing deep, embarrassing and intimate details about my life. Sometimes his life.

'Nothing dangerous for you,' I said.

'Then it's all fine.' He slammed it shut.

And it was. Until my book launch and talk when my dad was in the front row and a bored young father dragged there by his wife asked how I wrote the section on 'how to give a killer blowjob'.

'I did a lot of interviews,' I replied, face red, and not daring to glance at dad. Or mom.

TASK 26

How To Write About Yourself?

> 'No one will forget me. Not my look, not my name. Katniss. The girl who was on fire.'
> **Suzanne Collins, *The Hunger Games***

WRITING ABOUT YOURSELF IS AN exercise in both honesty and storytelling. You are narrating your own life or experience, but you are also the hero of a story. So the question is, how do you create this hero when it is YOU?

- ✓ How do you elevate yourself above being an ordinary person and into the realm of a literary character who people are inspired to read about?
- ✓ What if your story is not gripping enough to make you into this 'hero'?
- ✓ What if you don't want to be in your story at all?
- ✓ How will you hold their attention for 250 pages?
- ✓ How much of yourself should you really reveal?

The key to this is to see yourself as the hero of the book, and devise a character that is gripping and entertaining so that readers are willing to spend some time with you. Even if you are writing non-fiction, the readers are buying into you as the expert, who has lessons to share.

Show your dark side

A lot of writers start off thinking they are going to impart wisdom in a book. But no!

Nobody wants to read about a goodie-two-shoes. The key to a strong lead character is that you show more of your flaws than of your strengths. That means you need to be bad, angry, vindictive and preferably all of those. You need to make big mistakes.

Are you trying to paint yourself in a good light? Why? Readers relate to characters who struggle, get stuff wrong, make bad judgement calls and stuff it all up. Make sure you are NOT putting your best foot forward.

Readers want to read the real trials. The real hardships. They want to read about the moments when you were at your lowest ebb. Your worst behavior. This is the popularity of a memoir or the transformation of a non-fiction book. The reader wants to live out their worst fears, but through someone else. They don't need to be a crack addict; they can read your story. Show your arrogance, the pain you caused others, your abominable behavior and your deep questioning of life.

Get out your records

Memoirs need to be written with visual cues. Get out your photos of key events, client records, doctors' reports, letter, lawyers' communications, texts, and Facebook posts.

Can you include these actual documents?

What source material needs a place in your book?

You must talk

Talk to other people, talk to yourself, talk to the reader. Reveal yourself through your dialogue—not only your thoughts.

Highlight a quirk

Choose something you habitually do and make more of it—perhaps it's an annoying habit, an amusing quirk, an obsession or a personality style. Don't share everything about yourself, just unique aspects. Jason Bourne is an obsessive map reader. Jack Reacher lives on the road with a toothbrush as his only constant. Find a small thing you do and develop it into a character trait. You may be OCD, an exercise fanatic, like to do stand-up comedy, pound the pavement and run late at night, bake when you are stressed, glug down tequila with your mates, secretly work as a vigilante, carry a Glock. The point is, choose one vivid detail and make it part of your character build.

WRITING TASK

Write a scene in which another character sums you up. They can be talking to you, or to someone else. What are they saying about you? How do you feel? Can you include interior dialogue? Can you anchor in body language so we understand not just how you feel, but where you are.

Complete these sentences about yourself:

- I hate …
- I never …
- I refuse …
- I can tell you …
- I am terrible at …

HEART TASK

One simple idea for you today. What is the ONE question you need to be asking yourself right now about your book that will take you and your writing to the next level?

Some examples might be:

- Am I being honest?
- Why am I really writing this book?
- What is truly blocking me?
- Why am I sabotaging myself again?
- Have I put 100% effort into this?
- Whose help do I most need?
- Am I ready to share my words with the world?
- How can I up the ante and reach my deadline?

Find YOUR question and allow yourself to answer it with the vulnerability and honesty that will make you a better writer. Write out your question and answer and stick it up somewhere visible.

TASK 27

Where's the Conflict?

> 'The only thing more unthinkable than leaving was staying; the only thing more impossible than staying was leaving.'
>
> **Elizabeth Gilbert, *Eat, Pray, Love***

HUH? I HEAR YOU GROAN. That word again. Why must you have conflict in this kind of book? Isn't that for novels?

Well conflict no, is not just for novels. All books are about a struggle. But is that stuggle making it onto paper?

Human life sure is. Professional life sure is. It is just filled with misunderstandings, bad moods, thwarted longings, unreturned crushes, scrappy fights, ignored texts, emails sent to the wrong person, tactless moments, horrid bosses and drunken boo-boos.

In fact these moments dominate. That is why we have to force ourselves to write those 10 gratitudes in a journal, right? Life, or a good story, is made up of more wrongs than a right. Those are the good stories that people tell over dinner. Not them winning, but just how badly they lost.

So where are these fails in your book? Or are you just presenting the good vibes?

Any book is a story, not just a collection of your ideas, thoughts or memories. Most often people read a book to feel, be entertained or find information. Good stories only happen when you have structure and conflict.

Ask yourself this week as you write:
Do you have enough tortured emotion in your writing and do you spell that out literally to your reader (see the quote at the top of this task)?

Do you have a core central struggle (conflict) built into your book that the reader clearly understands is your personal and private battle? Is this struggle yours, someone else's or a concept you (or your readers) are battling with?

How would conflict unfold in a memoir?
Conflict is the core of all memoir. We are watching you—as hero—fight. You have to fight against a lot to grow, heal, live or become bigger. We want a litany of struggles. The more the better.

These could (and should) be:

- ✓ Other people – annoying people, challenging people, clever people, bosses, lovers, enemies, parents, colleagues, children, exes. They must all be working against you (or so you think). Make sure there are enough of them
- ✓ Real obstacles – like, no money, illness, drugs, detractors, accidents, life events, problems, self-doubt, emotions, alcohol, people, stumbling blocks, kidnappings, accidents, locked doors
- ✓ Miscommunications – these are key to providing conflict
- ✓ Your own sparkling personality – You are your own worst enemy in memoir, and sadly in life too. Just be bad yourself, just badder. You need to doubt, stress, rage, challenge, hide, cry, laugh, get mean, get revenge, drink, shout, bitch, moan, hit and hate. Conflict is both external (things that happen) and internal (your own s**t).

These elements of plotting come in many forms and should come up many times in your book. All of these things are there to provide something for you (the hero) to struggle against. Without conflict you are running the risk of a too-good Pollyanna story.

How would conflict unfold in non-fiction?_
Think about your readers. What conflicts or problems are they experiencing that are driving them to read this book?

Even chapter-based non-fiction has to have things that go wrong. But these things are not as linear as a story plot.

Most often you are dealing with:

- ✓ Disagreeable people (clients, case studies, colleagues)
- ✓ Challenging ideas or theories
- ✓ Confronting incidents
- ✓ Your own struggles as expert or author
- ✓ Struggles others have encountered that you can share.

Remember the argument you set up in the beginning of your book?

- Are you interrogating that?
- Are you being controversial enough?
- Are you sharing difficult parts of your own journey?
- Are you challenging people to change their lives/minds/diets/thinking/friends? Who is challenging you—your argument/theory/life/lessons/sanity/family/self-esteem/sales?

Part of understanding conflict is lifting your head out of your life, your thoughts and your story and asking … is this book engaging for a reader? And how can I add another level of conflict and action? Am I just rolling out my theory without any color, challenges or confrontations?

WRITING TASK

This week you are going to be Bad to the Bone.

Take a good look at your planning documents.
Are you giving your book enough of these elements?
Are you being too nice, clean, tidy and perfect?
Are you addressing the problems your readers have?

In all the sections you write this week up the ante on conflict. Write only about nasty people and nasty things. We want to feel your desperation. No room for bland emotions in this book.

- An angry dialogue
- A bad client
- Bad behavior (by you, clients or other characters)
- Screw-ups (made by you, clients or other characters)
- A bad attitude – unapologetically so
- An example of when you messed up and didn't apologize (or make it all nice).

Can you include all?

TASK 28

Make a List

> 'The secret of it all, is to write in the gush, the throb, the flood, of the moment—to put things down without deliberation—without worrying about their style—without waiting for a fit time or place. I always worked that way. I took the first scrap of paper, the first doorstep, the first desk, and wrote—wrote, wrote … By writing at the instant the very heartbeat of life is caught.'
>
> **Walt Whitman**

AHHH, A CLEAR AND CONCISE list. I love them. Readers love them. Publishers love them.

You should love them, and use them to great effect in your book.

- List and cut out all the extra words
- They clarify and reduce
- They prioritize
- They can bring a different tone to your book
- They can shift into humor quickly, and are a great device for including this
- They can sum up an entire chapter and remind readers of your key points or lessons
- They are a great way to deliver a lot of information fast.

Your entire non-fiction book or memoir is actually a list of key points (called chapters or scenes). One by one, you will tick these off your list as you write them.

Examples:

- ✓ 10 things never to say to a toddler
- ✓ 15 ways to make him want more
- ✓ Three ways to improve your business fast
- ✓ 10 dangers you don't know are lurking in your kitchen
- ✓ The seven mistakes I made in my marriage.

Lists are also a great way to condense your book and think ahead to create a compelling blog or magazine article.

Make a list of:

- Lessons you've learned in this journey
- Mistakes you've made/people make
- Things most people get wrong (in your topic)
- The biggest myths about (your topic)
- What not to do or say.

HEART EXERCISE

Give yourself permission to keep going—step by step.

Are you now writing as much as you can, as often as you can, fully immersed? Remember to ENJOY every step of this early process, no matter how many times you fall off the wagon. You can, of course, take as long as you need on this journey, but we want you to finish your first draft in 100 days. So you need to really make each week count. Keep going!

Word by word.
Sentence by sentence.
Paragraph by paragraph.
Scene by scene.
A first draft.

Yes, it's kind of that simple!
And that hard.

YOUR WORD COUNT TARGET IS 45,000 WORDS

Keep writing now to get to 50,000 words as a minimum. You can write to 80,000.

TASK 29

How Does Your Story End?

> 'I like non-fiction books about people with wretched lives.'
>
> **David Sedaris**

SO IF YOU ARE HONESTLY doing the work, you should be into the last part of your book. Ideally you are working on 45,000 words and cracking on to get to your target of 50,000.

This task may feel premature to you right now, but now I want you to write two key scenes in your book as you move to the finish line.

The first is the turnaround scene
The second in the last scene of your book

A turnaround scene needs to:

- ✓ Show the reader a tough decision you need to make to bring an appropriate end to your story
- ✓ Reveal the courage this will take
- ✓ End with a clear plan of action
- ✓ Be steeped in pure emotion.

Here's an example to inspire you of using strong emotion in personal writing from *A Child Called It,* by Dave Pelzer

> *Standing alone in that damp, dark garage I knew, for the first time, that I could survive. I decided that I would use any tactic I could think of to defeat Mother or to delay her from her grisly obsession. I knew if I wanted to live, I would have to think ahead. I could no longer cry like a helpless baby. In order to survive, I could never give in to her. That day I vowed to myself that I would never, ever again give that bitch the satisfaction of hearing me beg her to stop beating me.*

An end scene needs to:

- ✓ Close out or bring an appropriate end to the story
- ✓ Satisfy the reader on an emotional level. Whether you leave them on a romantic high, reeling from a breathless fight to the death, or grabbing for the tissues, the ending must just feel RIGHT
- ✓ Keep your promise. If you promised a search for a cure, give a solution. If you promised answers, are they delivered? If you promised an inspirational story, can you end with insight and growth?
- ✓ Tie up most of the major plot lines and answer the questions you raised in the book
- ✓ Have an element of looking back. There is an emotional component to the end of a book. It's been a long journey. It hints at the future. It understands the past.

The end may echo the start on an emotional level or metaphoric level—often using imagery we encountered at the beginning. We have come full circle, but we have fundamentally changed. You have been on an adventure, you have emerged a hero. But we remember that person we met 300 odd pages ago.

Here's how Sharon Osborne ended her gripping memoir *Extreme!*

'I know it's hard for people to understand how, after all I have gone through with my husband, I am still here. I am because I love him, and, apart from my children—who he gave me—Ozzy is the only person in my entire life who has ever loved me. Fat, thin, crazy, horrible, it doesn't matter. His love is unconditional. And when he doesn't have his demons on his shoulder, he is the sweetest, funniest, loveliest, most caring man in the world, and Ozzy's demons are getting weaker and weaker. He has matured so much and grown so much over the past year, and he's bettered his life. Now it's my turn to work to change my behaviors. For the last twenty-something years I have made all the decisions in our life together, I was holding his hand; now it's time for him to hold mine.'

'Sharon?'
There he is now, coming up the stairs.
'Yeseeee!'
'What are you doing? We're all waiting for you.'
'I'm coming down. Just having a bit of a think.'
He wanders into the room.
'Nothing bad, eh, Shaz?'
'No, Ozzy. Nothing bad. I was just packing,' and I smile at him, looking so worried, pushing a curtain of hair behind his ear, something I must have watched him do ten thousand million times before. And he smiles back at me. A smile that could light up a room.
'I love you, Mama.'
'And I love you, Dada. Now come over here and give us a kiss.'
Extreme! My Autobiography, **Sharon Osbourne**

WRITING TASK

As you move to the end you are going to write BOTH of the scenes detailed here. These scenes are not action driven, they are pure emotion. These are also shorter than your more action-driven scenes. Aim for 800 words.

HEART EXERCISE

As you think about the end of your story today, you might start noticing all sorts of self-limiting beliefs. A kind of panic might set in about what if you can't fill in the rest of the words that take you all the way to the end? Totally normal!

Writing and completing your first draft is less about skill and talent, and far more about managing all the nonsense whirling around in your head and heart. That is the real stuff that will throw you off track and shove you down the rabbit hole of 'who the hell am I to write this book?' Or 'who will actually care?' You really are well into the writing process now, and there will probably be some days when it all goes belly up! If it hasn't yet tripped you up, you might start grappling with …

- Possible resistance in the face of your end goal
- Procrastination regarding your regular bum time
- 'Busyness' with everything else OTHER than your writing. Nurglies, demons and monsters that rear their head and question every word you write
- The constant mind babble and self-deprecating voice, aka the inner critic we spoke about in Task 20
- Feeling that your goal of completing your first draft is

impossible and unattainable

- The overwhelming feeling that hits you hard in your solar plexus in the middle of the night.

What to do, what to do?

Sometimes you have to let yourself off the hook a little. Change your routine, do some exercise to get the blood flowing, or do something that totally distracts you for a while, such as binge-watching a series for three hours.

But at some point you have to reel yourself back in again and lean in harder, write to shorter and tighter deadlines, and literally march yourself to your computer and write just one more scene. One. Then the next one. Flow will return.

You have to be willing to engage the level of your heart and mind in this process. Call in your support system and perhaps book a mentoring session to help you move through and beyond any of the obstacles that come out to sabotage you. It's important to remember that they WILL try to do this, for sure. So how are you going to tackle them when they do? Perhaps today is about reaching out?

TASK 30
Refine Your Title and Subtitle

> 'When you write non-fiction, you sit down at your desk with a pile of notebooks, newspaper clippings, and books and you research and put a book together the way you would a jigsaw puzzle.'
> **Janine di Giovanni**

YOU ARE MUCH CLEARER NOW about your book. Can you improve your book title now to make it better, tighter and more focused? Most books have both a title and a subtitle.

The title and subtitle work together.
The title catches a reader's attention.
The subtitle clarifies exactly what the book is about.

Your book title and subtitle together need to fulfil a few roles:

- ✓ Immediately hook your reader
- ✓ Shine a light on your story's theme or controlling idea
- ✓ Set out exactly what your book is about
- ✓ Make a promise to those readers
- ✓ Appeal to as wide a readership as possible without alienating the core genre fans
- ✓ Create an authorial sensibility, if this is your first work of fiction or non-fiction, or abide by an already established authorial sensibility. This means it needs to fit with your other titles if you have other books already!

Here are some clear, tight examples to inspire you.

- *Everything I Never Wanted to Be: A Memoir of Alcoholism and Addiction, Faith and Family, Hope and Humor* by Dina Kucera
- *Beyond the Blues: A Workbook to Help Teens Overcome Depression* by Lisa M. Schab
- *Priceless: How I Went Undercover to Rescue the World's Stolen Treasures* by Robert K. Wittman
- *Look Me in the Eye: My Life with Asperger's* by John Elder Robison
- *Eat, Pray, Love: One Woman's Search for Everything Across Italy, India and Indonesia* by Elizabeth Gilbert
- *The Color of Water: A Black Man's Tribute to His White Mother* by James McBride
- *Getting to Yes! Negotiating Agreement without giving in* by Roger Fisher and William Ury
- *Air Babylon: A Mile-high Journey through the Best-kept Secrets of the Airline Industry* by Imogen Edwards-Jones & Anonymous
- *Romance 101! Can your Relationship Survive your Kids (and Other Passion Killers)?* by Sarah Bullen

Kate's book titles work together as a body of work that reinforce her author brand. It has been a deliberate choice over the years.

- *Clear Your Clutter: A practical, no-nonsense book that teaches you the WHY and the HOW of ridding yourself of emotional, physical and body clutter*
- *Ditch Your Glitch: A purposeful journey to face your 'glitch' An honest process to Step in, Step up and Step out*
- *Shift Your Home: The Power of Closure, Clarity and Clearing to Shift your Heart and Sell your Home*

WRITING TASK

Write four totally different versions of the title for your book idea. They must have a title AND a subtitle.

Go and look at a bookshop to see how others have done it. Share your top three on our author Facebook group to get some feedback.

P.S. Sometimes your favorite idea leaves others feeling bleh. And that one you want to ditch is the one that 'pops' for your readers.

Task 31
How Is It All Working Out for You?

> 'We have to continually be jumping off cliffs and developing our wings on the way down.'
> **Kurt Vonnegut**

ARE YOU OVERWHELMED OR UNDERWHELMED right now? Neither is totally ideal.

Every time you sit down to write, plan or plot, start off by taking 10 deep breaths while tuning in to your inspirational WHY. Get centered, get clear.

By now you are well into your book and inching towards your mega deadline.

Let's do an essential check in. You should have:

- ✓ A long, evolving and growing list of your key chapters or scenes of your book
- ✓ Written at least 40,000 words and are heading to 50,000—no matter how bleh, cringe-worthy or inadequate they feel to you
- ✓ A big notebook of ideas or a visual representation of your book.

BUT

- ✓ What if you haven't?
- ✓ What if you haven't written a word? Or only 4,000 words?

- ✓ What if you have simply been 'organizing' your information?
- ✓ What if you have thought a LOT about it, but not written much?
- ✓ What if you think what you have written is dreadful?
- ✓ What if you want to ditch this book, re-think it and start an entirely different one? What if you now have a better book, a better angle, or a better idea?

All of these thoughts are totally normal. All writers have them. Just keep moving through them.

If you are behind in your writing, don't panic entirely. But it is time to really change gear. You are in first gear, and you need to navigate very swiftly into third gear. This car does not work on automatic.

From a practical point of view, you are going to have to make up some words if you want to finish in 100 days from when you started—but you can schedule extra writing time. If you don't pull finger and get cracking now, you are not going to finish in your allotted time.

What if you don't finish on time? This (of course) is totally okay. This is a deadline YOU set. Nobody is standing cracking a whip over your head (except us). Nobody is going to punish you. And sure, we can have this conversation next year. We can talk about the book you WANT TO WRITE. The book you are BUSY WRITING. But I would prefer to be talking to you next year about your final edit. Your publishing contact, your review copies. Your book launch. Your first talk.

Dig deep, writers.

WRITING TASK

Today have some fun with your writing. Tell yourself you are simply going to throw words on the page. You are not going to care. Your only goal now is to get your word count rising fast.

HEART EXERCISE

Grab your journal right now and do a little personal writing reflection.

Make a list of all the hiccups/challenges/resistances that are rearing their heads.

Ask yourself if your writing intentions are getting shoved out the way.

- Are you allowing your weekly word count goals to be constantly negotiated?
- Is real life taking over and demanding your love and attention? (This stuff is vital and sometimes means that your writing takes a back seat for a while—and that's okay!)
- Are you self-sabotaging and falling into old, pesky habits?
- Are you saying one thing, yet somehow doing another?
- Have found your own writing rhythm?
- Are you at your best in the morning, evening, snippets of time in between other demands, or looooong stretches?

Now get practical and pick one or two that resonate from the list below to get back on track today!

- Schedule MORE bum time. Either longer or more often
- Change the venue of your regular bum time to spice it up
- Or write somewhere else in your home for a fresh perspective
- Bend your buddy's ear. Or find a buddy if you don't have one
- Stop reading other authors' books and write your own
- Quit talking about your book and start writing your book NOW
- Quickly calculate how many words you need to write per week to meet the deadline you set way back at the beginning. Stick it up on your wall
- Go back to basics—what is your big WHY? Why are you doing this again?
- Think about the moment in the future when you get to hold YOUR book in your hands for the first time. IN PRINT. Whoaaaaaa!
- Meditate on your long-held dream of being an author
- Walk to your computer now and write ONE more scene!

TASK 32

Refocus Your Book With a Tight One-Pager

> 'I read almost exclusively non-fiction when I read, because even though it's harder to find a great true story, when you find one, the idea that it actually happened is immensely powerful. That's what moves me the most.'
>
> **Robert Kurson**

DON'T STOP THE FORWARD DRIVE of your word count. That is your primary goal here. But as you continue to write, you are going to create a tight and clever one-pager about your book. It needs to be a clear, executive-type high-level summary about this book, much like you would find in a well-crafted business plan. It is also key to refocus you and your book idea. Don't take too long on this one—it is a fast and furious task. Just fling it down.

It should be no more than one typed page or 400 words.

Give it

- ✓ A good working title and subtitle
- ✓ Clearly state your genre
- ✓ It should present your BIG IDEA, ARGUMENT or your WHY.

It must include:

- ✓ Just tell us in simple terms what it is about. Include all spoilers. Cut out all the fluff.
- ✓ Your professional expertise is critical. Why are you an expert?
- ✓ What's the outcome and why should anyone care?
- ✓ Who should read this book and what will the reader get out of it?

WRITING TASK

Write your one-pager now. Take no longer than 20 minutes to condense all your information into this simple document. You can write this in first person or third person (see example below).

THEN

Can you tighten it all up a bit further into the very best few sentences you can possibly craft? This is the teaser on the back of your book that is going to make a reader buy it.

An example (in 3rd person):

Lost Connections: Why You're Depressed and How to Find Hope by Johann Hari

Depression and anxiety are now at epidemic levels. Why? Across the world, scientists have uncovered evidence for nine different causes. Some are in our biology, but most are in the way we are living today.

Lost Connections *offers a radical new way of thinking about this crisis. It shows that once we understand the real causes, we can begin to turn to pioneering new solutions—ones that offer real hope.*

There was a mystery haunting award-winning investigative journalist Johann Hari. He was thirty-nine years old, and almost every year he had been alive, depression and anxiety had increased in Britain and across the Western world. Why?

He had a very personal reason to ask this question. When he was a teenager, he had gone to his doctor and explained that he felt like pain was leaking out of him, and he couldn't control it or understand it. Some of the solutions his doctor offered had given him some relief—but he remained in deep pain.

So, as an adult, he went on a forty-thousand-mile journey across the world to interview the leading experts about what causes depression and anxiety, and what solves them. He learned there is scientific evidence for nine different causes of depression and anxiety—and that this knowledge leads to a very different set of solutions: ones that offer real hope.

YOUR WORD COUNT TARGET IS 50,000 WORDS

TASK 33

Should You Change Your 'oint of View?

> 'When they kick out your front door
> How you gonna come?
> With your hands on your head
> Or on the trigger of your gun?'
> **The Clash**

WE ARE IN THE FINAL push now. Write, write and write some more. Drink more coffee if you have to and gallons and gallons of water to stay hydrated. It may be that you have been writing without giving much thought to the technical side of the craft. Let's change that and have some fun with playing with viewpoint.

You have probably been writing in the first person. That is the default style of most writers, and the correct way to write a memoir.

First-person	I/we
Second-person	you/you
Third-person	he/she

Second-person narration is also effective at times.

This is where you refer to YOURSELF as 'you'. Look at the example below.

> *You are not the kind of guy who would be at a place like this at this time of the morning. But here you are, and you cannot*

say the terrain is entirely unfamiliar although the details are fuzzy. You are at a nightclub talking to a girl with a shaved head. The club is either Heartbreak or the Lizard Lounge. All might come clear if you could just slip into the bathroom and do a little more Bolivian Marching Power.

***Bright Lights, Big City,* Jay McInerney**

- ✓ Too much **second-person** narration can be uncomfortable for the reader
- ✓ A publisher will recoil if you send a book written entirely in this style.
- ✓ Reserve it for a dream sequence, or a disembodied scene for particular effect.

Third-person omniscient/reportage is often used in a first chapter of a book or in a prologue. The viewpoint not only can see everything that is going on, but can also know what is going on in everyone's head.

Next challenging question: Are you actually in viewpoint at all?

You need to be aware of writing in viewpoint. This is also called POV (point of view) or VP writing. But what does this mean?

It means that your story can only be told through one person's eyes at a time. In a novel this is a choice. However, in a memoir this person is always you. In a memoir, the only way you can know what another character is thinking is through the dialogue, what they tell you, or their body language.

Think of your reader as a little person who rides inside the head of one of your characters. When inside a given head, the reader can see, hear, touch, smell, and taste everything that particular character is experiencing. The reader can also hear the thoughts of that one character. But they can't jump into another person's head.

> *I smiled at Jasmine. She was a total babe, with lips that begged to be kissed and a deliciously curvy figure.*

Okay, so we're settling in for an encounter with a woman from a man's point of view. But if the next paragraph says:

> *Jasmine smiled back, intrigued. He was a handsome man, with a body-builder's physique.*

Whoa! Wait a minute! Suddenly we've jumped into another head, and immersed ourselves in a different set of emotions and feelings. Not only have we lost track of who we are, but also of which character we're supposed to identify with.

WRITING TASK

Write a scene in the second person. This is where you refer to yourself as 'you'. Look at above example again.

You can use the following trigger sentences:

- You shouldn't be here …
- You know you are going to win …
- You know what they are going to tell you …
- You glide through the room …

TASK 34

Take Your Writing Craft Up a Notch

> 'Like all art, non-fiction film should invite, seduce, or force us to confront the most difficult, frightening or mysterious aspects of what it means to be human.'
>
> **Joshua Oppenheimer**

The five commandments of writing a 'age-turner

1. Avoid dead ends

When you write your scenes, remember that you must move from point A to point B. If the action or story or argument hasn't been advanced in some way, the scene doesn't belong in the book.

2. Don't try to resolve it all

Some forward action must continually be implied to drive the reader to turn the page. That means that if you have a scene that begins with you looking for your father's will, make sure you DON'T find it. Save that for another scene.

3. Make sure the party's already started

Don't start a scene in the beginning. Cut out the boring stuff. In Latin, it's called *medias res*—in the midst of things. If you know a certain scene is going to take place at a party, make sure you move into the scene only once it's all going. You don't have to describe yourself getting dressed, or driving there, or thinking about what to wear. Start the scene as you walk into the party, already in full swing. What is going to go wrong?

4. Set up a series of escalating obstacles

Set up an obstacle in one scene, but don't resolve it until a future scene. Don't resolve it, and then keep adding to the challenge. Let's take the example of a memoir about your trip on the Camino Santiago to get over your soul-stripping divorce. What will drive the plot is a series of obstacles (a massive blister that turns septic, an accident, being locked in an old church, a dog bites you, you lose your shoes). The reader must be rooting for you to finish the walk. Your goal is to walk 800 kilometres. The obstacles in your way will present the plot of the book. Make sure there are lots of them. Remember: These obstacles are not negative thoughts, but real challenges along the way.

5. Keep the number of players down

Don't bring someone into your book unless it is absolutely necessary and they drive your plot or argument onwards. When you overcomplicate a scene, or the reader is forced to spend unnecessary time on other characters, it breaks the narrative spell you are trying to cast. Earlier we suggested a cast of eight.

PS … Can you see how we just gave you a list, like we challenged you to do back in Task 28? Works, right?

WRITING TASK

Can you push yourself to the end of this week and write double your word count? Why not? Notice how your writing has naturally improved as your word count climbs. Set your sights higher. Be specific, set clear goals and clear time frames for each writing slot you do.

Task 35
Write To The End

> 'Begin at the beginning … and go on till you come to the end: then stop.'
> **Lewis Carroll**

YOUR ONLY JOB RIGHT NOW is to get to the end of your book. You need to be single-minded about this. Do not stop until you hit your word count. When you are there, that will be time to move on to Part 3 of this book. When you are done please come and share a screenshot of your word count on our accountability group. We need to see your success too!

HEART EXERCISE

Retreat time! While the notion of regular bum time is what moves your word count forward, bit by bit, we also know that life tends to gets in the way at every possible opportunity. We need to go up a notch now, and start contemplating longer IMMERSION times. We call this 'retreat' time.

These are longer pockets of time, typically two to seven days. They are non-negotiable dates blocked out in your diary. Retreat time has the sole aim of ramping up your word count by immersing yourself fully. Ideally it's somewhere quiet, inspirational, away from home, and with no wifi connection (unless you are honestly and truly doing research!). It could be with others on a structured writing retreat or a solo flight. It depends on your personality and what helps you to focus and dive deep. Do you need vibey city energy, clean mountain air, or sandy beach walks to energize you when you get up from your computer?

Yes, of course you can enter into 'retreat' mode at home: it just requires pre-shopping, pre-planning and alerting friends and family so you have as few distractions as possible. Your call. On the other hand, having somewhere special that you have chosen and paid for also increases commitment to actually doing it and actually writing!

Take a look at your diary, consider the writing deadline you are inching towards, and get that retreat time booked. Even if it's for a couple of months down the line, you will be so grateful for it.

kate says

My go-to choice is always to gaze at the sea (calm or wild) when on writing deadlines. Other environments can definitely energize me and I don't always have the opportunity to be at the sea to immerse in retreat time.

But I'm a beach gal at heart and that brings me the most joy and the fastest word count. I play games with myself to write a certain amount and then enjoy the reward of a swim or a walk.

Sarah says

I regularly book two full days in my diary to write. Do I go away? Not always, but I make sure to get out of the house. If I write at home I find myself suddenly cleaning the pool, weeding the garden or doing some eating—instead of writing. When I am on a deadline I clear the decks. I only turn on my phone in the evening and I write (or edit) until I get to the end. That is what it takes—and I will do whatever it takes. Not finishing is not an option.

'art Three
Your Author Brand

> 'The challenge in fiction is to write a terrific story. The challenge in journalism is to communicate solid, objective information. The challenge in creative non-fiction is to do it both and to do it well.'
>
> **Lee Gutkind**

IF YOU HAVE REACHED THIS point, you have either completely finished your first draft or you haven't. Black or white. Either way you have most certainly now have a good idea of what it really takes to write an entire book. It is a surprising amount of work, right?

Okay, time to breathe.

If you haven't finished your first draft you are going to find time to push to the end before you move forward. But first, if you have honestly been at it for the last 100 days, take a little break (even if just for this week).

- ✓ Think it through
- ✓ Then come back fighting strong, set a new date when you will finish this draft and put it in your diary
- ✓ Restart your Word Count Tracker
- ✓ Commit to it
- ✓ Build in rewards along the way
- ✓ What needs to be done differently now as you work towards the finish line?

If you have finished your first draft, then we hope you have already celebrated in some form. Have you shared it on the FB group?

It's a major accomplishment for every writer! You will walk the next steps down the path to publication. But not just yet! While you are waiting, and ignoring that manuscript, you are going to be working on the bigger picture of your brand as an author and how you want to send this book out into the world.

Sure, there are going to be errors, inconsistencies, plot holes, characters that don't work, subplots that do nothing to advance the plot and dialogue that is going to want to make you tear your hair out. That is totally normal. That's what the first draft is supposed to be. What you do have is step one of your book COMPLETED.

Do NOT send your book to friends, editors, publishers or buddies. We can't stress this enough. A first draft is an imposition to ask anyone to read. Don't Do It. In non-fiction you can get away with sending a second draft but we have very strict guidelines for that. Don't disperse the energy of your book too soon.

Here's what you ARE going to do now

Your only task now is to put your book aside.

Step 1: Print it. Print out a hard copy of your manuscript (MS). I usually do this at a print shop and get them to bind it. I print it single-sided so I can make copious notes on the blank left page. Don't waste money by printing with double spacing. Do put page numbers on it.

Step 2: Bag it. Then blow it a kiss and stick in it your drawer for at least a week, three weeks is even better. Don't even think of reading it now. Go do something else. Work on your author brand. Start blogging. Forget the book for a wee while.

Step 3: Shift all your energy now to Part 3 if you are serious about becoming a published author. There is plenty there to keep you busy!

Step 4: When it's time to come back to your book, get stuck into Part 4 to Edit like a Boss and get your Pitch Deck together! Exciting times ahead.

TASK 36
Create Your Author Brand with Tessa Graham

> 'A brand is a living entity—and it is enriched or undermined cumulatively over time, the product of a thousand small gestures.'
>
> **Michael Eisner, Former CEO Disney**

AS AUTHORS, WE NEED TO be savvier than ever about who reads our books. We have the ability to market our books directly to our readers. We no longer need to rely on agents, publishers and booksellers to get our message across and sell our books and our brand.

In the past, as an author, you would find an agent, the agent would find a publisher, and the publisher would take care of the editing, design, printing, marketing and distribution to booksellers and ultimately to the customers.

While that model still loosely exists today we now have the responsibility to create and build our own personal brands and to let the world know who we are and what we stand for.

The world of publishing is changing. Digital technology has turned it on its head. Authors are no longer just pictures and short bios on an inside back cover. They have websites, Facebook fan pages, Instagram followers; they Tweet, speak, conduct seminars and even sell products.

As an author, it is critical to create a unique, consistent, relevant and authentic brand.

To be truly authentic, your brand is based on YOU—your personality, values, vision, beliefs and everything that makes YOU truly unique! Most importantly, it is based on your WHY.

So let's get in to the flow of creating our brand by first of all understanding what a brand is.

Exercise 1 – Your favorite brands

What are your three favorite brands? You can choose a person, an author, a company, a product or a service—anything that you feel is relevant. Write them down.

Why are these your favorite brands? Note next to each one what about it draws you.

Do these have anything in common?

You might have said that you like the experience of the brand, that you like the product they offer, that you like their books as they are always gripping. No answer is the wrong answer.

Exercise 2 – What is a brand?

Name four things you believe a brand has.

What we all know is that a brand is more than a logo. It can be everything from a trademark, an experience, the music that is played, what something looks like, what posts are on social media, what a website looks like, and the tone of voice that is used.

> ***Brand – /brand/ – noun:***
> The sum of all of the experiences of a company, product, product service or person.

I love to use the example of Apple. The experience is defined by the product, the services, their website, their advertising as well as what happens when you go into an Apple store. It's not just one thing that defines the brand, but the sum of all of the experiences you have with it.

The same applies to you as an author. It's important to think about your brand and what the sum of all of the experiences of BRAND YOU is—to your readers, your editor, your publisher, your PR agent (if you have one)—and most importantly for you to understand what it is you stand for.

To build an authentic 'personal' brand, we need to have a deep understanding of who you are, what you stand for and, most importantly, your 'why'.

So the starting point is to define your brand by using a tool that I call the BrandPrint. It takes time, focus and dedication to put it together. In my experience, it is a critical step in the process of building your brand.

What is the BrandPrint?

- ✓ A one-page outline of the key elements that drill down into who you are—your brand 'soul'.
- ✓ It provides clarity, direction and meaning for everyone involved.
- ✓ It serves as a strategic platform for all decisions moving forward.
- ✓ It also assures that all activities and initiatives that you undertake support brand 'you'.

The BrandPrint is made up of eight key elements:

1. ***Brand personality***

A set of human character traits that personify who you are in the world.

2. ***Brand values***

One-word descriptions of the core principles you stand for.

3. ***Brand beliefs***

The beliefs are short statements that are the core tenets of truth that guide your actions.

4. ***Brand benefits***

The benefits are what people 'get' from you

5. ***Promise***

The promise is the meaningful and relevant pledge that your brand makes to everyone all of the time.

6. ***Vision***

What you see the world being once you have made your contribution.

7. ***Mission***

How you make your impact in the world.

8. ***Your WHY***

The foundation of your house. The WHY that motivates you to make a change in the world.

Exercise 3 – Define Your BrandPrint

Now it's time to get to work on your own brand.

First things first, set aside a good two-hour session to get started. It's always fun to do it with someone who knows you well—and it makes it an easier process.

There are eight parts to creating a single-page document that is your essential BrandPrint. Each one of these steps is asking you to get clearer on the 'soul' of your brand.

Work through the steps below. Take a clean sheet of paper and write down the words that really jump out at you.

Step 1: Your personality
Name the seven most relevant character traits that personify who you are.
*Look at List 4: Personality Traits in the Addendum.

Examples:
✓ Trustworthy
✓ Open-minded
✓ Passionate
✓ Proactive
✓ Visionary
✓ Empowering
✓ Intelligent

Step 2: Your values
Write down seven one-word descriptions of the core principles that speak to what you stand for. These are your personal values.
*Look at List 5: Personal Values in the Addendum.

Examples:

- ✓ Vision
- ✓ Teamwork
- ✓ Integrity
- ✓ Humility
- ✓ Wisdom
- ✓ Leadership
- ✓ Storytelling
- ✓ Sense of Humor.

Step 3: Your beliefs

Write down five to six short statements that are the core tenets of truth that guide you. These could be short expressions that you use often or quotes that you love.

Examples:

- ✓ All life is precious
- ✓ Focus on campaigns that define decisive victories
- ✓ Change happens when there is urgency and pressure
- ✓ Change is driven by individuals not institutions
- ✓ There is more to unite us than divide us.

Step 4: How others benefit

Articulate five key ways that people you come in to contact with benefit from who you are and what you do. They are usually written from the point of view of your audience.

Examples:

- ✓ I feel inspired when witnessing and understanding the need for regeneration in the world
- ✓ I feel free, safe and happy
- ✓ I feel a true sense of well-being
- ✓ Care, compassion and consciousness are infectious

- ✓ To witness the working regenerative processes gives me hope for our future.

Step 5: Your promise

Your promise is a short statement of what you promise in every interaction you have with anyone.

Example:

- ✓ Inspired clarity.

Step 6: Your vision

This is a well crafted but short statement about how your contribution will change the world—or at the very least your readers!

Example:

- ✓ Better food for everyone.

Step 7: Your mission

This articulates what you will do to see your vision happen.

Example:

- ✓ To inspire people around the world to preserve and protect our oceans.

Step 8: Find your why

This is your personal WHY you do what you do.

Example:

- ✓ Expanding consciousness.

Now that you have defined the 'soul' of your brand, it should influence every decision you make in building your brand.

TASK 37

How To Build Awareness of Brand You with Tessa Graham

> 'We are defined as much by what we say no to as what we say yes to.'
> **Tessa Graham**

AS WE HAVE DISCOVERED, A brand is more than just a logo. It is the sum of all of the experiences that a person has with a company, product service or person.

Now that you have defined your brand and what you stand for, it is important to assure that this 'soul' informs everything that you do in building your brand. This is paramount to building an authentic brand based on your personality, values, vision, mission and WHY!

What is a brand?

Your BrandPrint is the soul that must inform all decisions moving forward in order to assure that the brand that you are building is in line with your authentic you!

So where do we start in building your brand? With the name!

As an author of a memoir or of a non-fiction book, it is likely to be one of the following:

- ✓ Your name – like Michelle Obama
- ✓ A pseudonym – like Robert Galbraith aka J.K. Rowling
- ✓ A character – like Harry Potter
- ✓ The name of your book or philosophy – like *Start With Why* by Simon Sinek

It is important to decide and choose one. You want to focus your efforts and resources on building one primary brand not on building a number of brands.

Exercise 1 – Hone in on the name of your brand

What is the 'NAME' of your brand? Get clear and write this down.

Once you have decided on the name of your brand, the next thing to do is secure your domain as well as the relevant social media handles.

It is important to be consistent and use the same name across all so that people can find you. If your domain name is brenebrown.com yet your Instagram handle is @vulnerablebeing, it will be harder for people to find you. So it's best to use the same name everywhere.

Exercise 2 – Secure your domain

In securing your domain, where your website will sit, which will also the domain for your email address, I suggest choosing a non-country specific version—not a .co.za or a .co.uk but rather a .com or a .me. The world is your oyster and by choosing a broader high-level domain, from a positioning perspective it makes you appear to be more global.

It is very inexpensive to secure your domain and usually costs less than $10 a year. Go Daddy is a great place to start: www.godaddy.com.

In an ideal world you should secure your name + .com. For example, Simon Sinek's primary domain is www.simonsinek.com. He has a secondary domain that points to this called *Start with Why*, the name of his bestselling book.

So, go forth and log on to www.godaddy.com or a similar service provider. Now, that you have decided on the name of your brand, see what domains are available. If your name is John Smith, it might already be gone. So you could use variations such as john-smith.com, johnsmithwriter.com or something similar.

What is the domain that you have secured?

Exercise 3 – Secure your social media handles

While there are new social media platforms popping up all the time, these are the key ones at the moment:

- ✓ Instagram
- ✓ Facebook
- ✓ YouTube
- ✓ Twitter.

There is no cost to secure your 'handle' on any of these platforms. Just be sure to secure the same name as your url or something very similar. Then register the same one across all platforms.

Even if you don't think you are going to use every one of them do it anyway. Better safe than sorry!

Now record the relevant details in a safe place.

Exercise 4 – Craft your social media bio

It's time for you to get writing about you! Each of these platforms allows you to include a bio. Look back on your BrandPrint and write two versions of your bio:

- ✓ 3–5 words (Instagram and Twitter)
- ✓ 150–300 words (YouTube and Facebook)

Have a go! Run them past someone whose opinion you trust to see if it reflects your true you, your brand and your WHY.

Now post them on the various platforms:

- ✓ Instagram
- ✓ Facebook
- ✓ YouTube
- ✓ Twitter.

Exercise 5 – Set up your author profile

While this is similar to the above exercise, you will also need to set up your Author Profile on:

- ✓ Goodreads
- ✓ Amazon
- ✓ LinkedIn.

You can sign in to each of these platforms and set it up accordingly. Have a look at examples that other authors you respect have used to give you a bit of inspiration.

When you are done, put a check mark next to each of these.

- ✓ Goodreads
- ✓ Amazon
- ✓ LinkedIn.

Exercise 5 – Get a professional profile picture taken

Having a professional headshot taken is very important. It is what the Swoosh is to Nike! It becomes your recognizable icon that can be used across all social media platforms as well as on your website.

It is worth the investment to get a professional photographer as they understand lighting, backdrops and will make you look your best. It is also recommended to get a make-up artist in. It makes a big difference to the end result.

Make sure that your photos are 'on brand' and speak to your BrandPrint. If Brand You is casual, relaxed and funky, then dress accordingly. If you are more serious, passionate and innovative, then take that into consideration.

Your exercise is to research portrait photographers—online or by asking friends and colleagues—and make an appointment to get them done.

Exercise 6 – Your brand look and feel

Creating a consistent and recognizable brand look and feel can be slightly daunting and it is often best to get a designer involved. The elements that need to be considered are as follows and you can use this to brief the designer:

- ✓ Your logo
- ✓ The fonts
- ✓ Your brand colors
- ✓ How this all applies to:
    - Website, social media, avatars, backgrounds, posts, book cover and design.

Be sure to share your BrandPrint with them so they know exactly what you stand for. They can then put these words into a visual language.

Step 1: Put together a brief to the designer as to exactly what you are looking for them to do.

Step 2: Get a costing back from them and determine if it is within your budget.

Step 3: Have them start designing.

Exercise 7 – Build your online presence

Building a website can be an expensive exercise—but it doesn't have to be. Squarespace is immensely easy to use and you can build it yourself. Alternatively, if you have the budget you can hire an agency or designer to do it for you.

Plan it out before you start designing. First, decide on the navigation and what information you want to include. Then write all of the words that will be included.

A typical author website would include the following:

- ✓ Author bio
- ✓ About your book/books
- ✓ Link to purchase
- ✓ Social media links
- ✓ Blog / Latest news
- ✓ Testimonials
- ✓ Contact details.

Most importantly, keep it simple!

- ✓ Decide if you are going to do it yourself or get a designer on board. Establish your budget and research who can help you to get your site live
- ✓ Write the necessary content that will be used on your site
- ✓ Get the assets ready – including your headshot and any other relevant information that will be used
- ✓ Get building!

Exercise 8 – What's your communication strategy?

Now that you have all these channels, what on earth are you going to put on them? In fancy terms, this is your 'Communication Strategy'.

- Refer back to your BrandPrint and your WHY. Write a short list of five key areas on what you have 'permission' to talk about, the things that matter to you and what people will connect with

  For example, if you are a chef, you have 'permission' to talk about:
  ✓ Food
  ✓ Cooking
  ✓ Inspiration (travel, other chefs)
  ✓ Recipes.

- Look at what other authors and individuals are doing that you are inspired by. Write a list of ideas that you can use.

The great thing about digital media is that you don't need to be perfect! Don't get perfection paralysis. Just give it a go. The more you do it, the better you will get.

Exercise 9 – Time is your most precious commodity

Time is your most precious commodity. Spend it well. It should be focused on doing three things:

✓ Being commercial
✓ Building awareness
✓ Creating inspiration.

Keep track of how you spend your time and make sure you spend it wisely. Find the balance between these three areas. Being commercial will give you the resources you need to fulfil your why. Building awareness will make sure that other people know about it, and creating inspiration will make sure that you always have the energy.

The most important thing to remember in building your brand is assuring that everything you do, every book you write, ever post you load on social media, every opportunity that you pursue is aligned with Brand You!

TASK 38

Write and Rewrite Your Author Blurb

> 'Who is Malala? The gunman demanded.
> I am Malala and this is my story.'
> **Malala Yousafzai**

AN AUTHOR BLURB IS AN essential part of getting your book out there. It will form part of your book proposal/synopsis—the final document you are going to send to publishers if you want to present your book idea to them. Your task is to write yours this week for your proposal and media pack. It is part of what we call your 'PITCH DECK', which we are going to do in the next section.

Your author blurb is the one thing that all writers need to practise. It is part of building your larger brand. Writing a good one that sums up your personality, qualifications and book in a few succinct words is unbelievably useful for so many reasons.

Where will you use your blurb?

- ✓ It will end up on the cover or inside cover of your book
- ✓ It will be used in all marketing communications for publicity for your book
- ✓ You can use it on your blog/website/CV
- ✓ You can submit it to Wikipedia/LinkedIn as your page profile
- ✓ You can use it on your Amazon/Goodreads author page.

General format to use:

- ✓ *Sentence 1:* Include your name and surname along with two tight adjectives – this is your core identity or qualities
- ✓ *Sentences 2– 4:* How you have lived this story. Give a short list as to what is going to support this story
- ✓ *Sentence 5:* What is this going to reveal in the book?

Example 1 – Non-fiction (inspirational)

Resilience from the Heart by Gregg Braden

> *Scientist Gregg Braden realized early in his career that neither science nor spirituality could provide a complete picture of how to live the best life. He has traveled the world for over 30 years visiting some of the most pristine, undisturbed and remote places around the globe in an effort to glean the wisdom of our ancestors so he could combine it with cutting-edge science. The result of what he learned is found in this book.* Resilience from the Heart *is written with you in mind. Within these pages, you'll find everything you need to embrace the biggest challenges in life and do so in a healthy way.*

Example 2 – Memoir (inspirational)

My Surgeon Talks to Angels: A Journey From Science to Faith by Dr Veerle Van Tricht

> *Dr Veerle Van Tricht is a highly specialized eye surgeon who has spent most of her professional life working to restore vision. However, she has a vision of a different kind. Born into a cold Flemish family, Veerle knew at an early age that she had a connection with angels and the spirit world. In her 20-year career as a specialist surgeon, Dr V has been guided by her angelic helpers to save the sight of patients across the globe. This book will show you how she developed her gifts,*

and share with you some methods to develop your own.

Example 3 – Non-fiction (health)

It Works for Me by Noeleen Bridle

> *Noeleen Bridle used to be a top athlete. Today she runs her own gym and through trial and error, and by applying logic and research, she has developed a correct eating strategy for each of the three prevalent body types found in women and men. As a lifestyle consultant working with female clients she is actively involved in helping others change their lifestyles.*

Example 4 – Memoir (celebrity)

Extreme! by Sharon Osborne

> *Sharon Osborne was born in London in 1952. She is married to rock legend Ozzy Osbourne and has three children.*

'art four
Edit, 'olish, 'ublish

> 'I would write a book, or a short story, at least three times—once to understand it, the second time to improve the prose, and a third to compel it to say what it still must say. Somewhere I put it this way: first drafts are for learning what one's fiction wants him to say. Revision works with that knowledge to enlarge and enhance an idea, to reform it. Revision is one of the exquisite pleasures of writing.'
>
> **Bernard Malamud**

OKAY, WRITER—SOON-TO-BE AUTHOR—YOU have done your first draft. You have put it away and let it simmer for a while. You are thinking about Brand You.

So what next?

You are going to whip that rough first draft into a better second draft. Then perhaps even into a clean third draft.

We are going to walk you through the next steps and tell you what you need to do, and prepare, to send your book off to publishers.

Although we have suggested a timeline for you, we do know this may take you longer. Do not rush this phase. Make sure you have the absolute best version of your book before you send it off. Make sure your Pitch Deck will knock their socks off.

Work the copy. Edit. Fix. Refine.

The good news is that you have got the first iteration of YOUR BOOK.

Task 39

How To Read and Edit Your First Draft

> 'Write hard, write fast.
> Edit slow, edit tough,
> with a process both clear and cool.'
> ***The Art of War for Writers*, James Scott Bell**

IF YOU DIDN'T DO THIS at the end of Part 2, the first step now is to get a hard-copy (printed) version of your book. But please make sure you don't rush to do the next editing step. You absolutely need to walk away from the first draft of your book for at least three weeks. This will allow you to see it with 'fresh eyes' when you finally pick it up again.

Why? As you write you are too immersed in the detail. Your job now as you edit will be to step back and take a bigger look at the entire piece of work.

You are going to print your entire manuscript (MS) single-sided and get it bound. Do this at a printer and get them to bind it with a plastic ring binder with a clear plastic cover. Make sure you have page numbers on your MS and oodles of blank white paper on the left to write all your notes.

Never do a read-through on your screen. This will not work.

When you have this printed version in your hands you are going to tackle it systematically. You are going to do this:

- ✓ Sit down and read your entire book from start to finish, but only once. You need to do this read-through thoroughly. There is a limit to how many times you can read your own work. Your single task is to focus on making all the notes that you are going to action over the next few weeks.
- ✓ Make copious notes all over the manuscript. These can be huge structural changes, copy edits and typos, inconsistencies or anything you notice.

Things like:

- BORING BORING BORING this section lags
- Change this totally!
- Rewrite whole section as dialogue
- Repetition
- Who is this person? ... No introduction to them at all
- Move this to the end of the book
- This feels preachy
- Red hair! Said it was black earlier
- SLOW needs pace
- No clue what is happening here.

- ✓ Keep a series of left-hand-side (blank) pages where you keep notes of bigger stuff—general impressions, big mistakes, structural changes and overall mood and pace ideas. Make as many notes as you can and as detailed as you can.
- ✓ Use different colored pens for different notes (structure versus. tone). Add Post-it notes all over. This should end up looking like a very colorful document. Think of yourself as an engineer. You are going in to fix a project so make all the notes you need to do that.

Your biggest challenge?

This is going to be to STOP YOURSELF from making ANY of these changes on your manuscript while you are reading and making your notes. Whatever you do, DO NOT dash to your computer and try to fix any problems until you have read the entire thing and followed all the steps. You will try to fix something in Chapter 3 that may have no relevance to the overall story arc. You are reading like an editor and looking at the big picture. You are looking at pace, structure and story flow.

TASK 40

Editing Your Book – Round Two

> 'I think I did pretty well, considering I started out with nothing but a bunch of blank paper.'
> **Steve Martin**

YOUR NEXT STEP IS TO get back on your computer and start to fix all the errors you so carefully noted in the last task.

It is in the editing phase that you are going to slow down, see what you have, take stock and make it infinitely better.

You will intensify the conflict, tighten dialogue (or add it in), cut random characters or scenes, insert some scenes, clear up timelines and fix glaring errors. The aim is to make it better, tighter, more compelling, more focused and more publishable.

Some things to note:

Ignore spelling mistakes and typos. This is not the time for a copy edit and that will come at the very end of all your rewrites. We know it's hard, but don't get hung up on those smaller details yet.

Only tackle the big stuff. If you can see a huge plot hole, start with that. You may find you lack a strong subplot, or the book just doesn't make sense. There is no point in fixing your character's physical descriptions or small inconsistencies when the whole story is not making any sense.

You need to be ruthless. Clean it up. Pare it down. Cut out any duplication. Cut any unnecessary descriptions. Cut anything that does not push your story forward. Cut out characters or stories that leave you wondering – erm … what's the point of that again? Write in plain, clean English. If in doubt, leave it out.

Work steadily and systematically. You are working through your notes with an editor's eye. Be consistent and steadily build a better book.

You need to finish up. Give yourself a tight deadline by which to finish this edit. Set a clear goal. Ideally your edit takes no longer than two weeks. You can spend the next 10 years changing and improving your book. It may always be a dud. It may be a masterpiece. There are only so many rewrites you can do, and now we need to move forward to a point when you can send your book to a publisher.

Make a reminder list. These are things you have noticed about your writing in general. It can be what it needs, what it is lacking, or what you feel you want to work on. These can be on Post-it notes that you stick on your desk, but make sure you can see them the entire time you work on your rewrite.

Your list could look something like this:

- ✓ Emotion emotion emotion!
- ✓ More dialogue
- ✓ What's the cliffhanger?
- ✓ What's the solution?
- ✓ Stop waffling
- ✓ WTAF is going on here?

KEY POINT

You are now rewriting your manuscript. Most wannabee writers never get to this point! You are going to do this again and again until you get to the final version. We suggest you do at least three rewrites before you get to a point where this is your best version of your book. Then you may want to send it off to a trusted 'beta' reader to give you feedback as you move ahead with the next few steps.

TASK 41

Write a Killer Logline

> 'At the still point, there the dance is.'
> **T. S. Eliot, *Four Quartets***

WE ARE SHIFTING GEAR NOW and lifting our heads up from the editing and rewriting into a whole new phase on the journey of becoming an author. We are about to shift from writer into sales person.

You are going to write a LOGLINE for your book. This is a concept that has trickled through from movies but is commonplace now in book publishing. It is similar to an 'elevator pitch' in which you sum up your entire book in one sentence.

It may be the answer you give at a family event when they ask you (again) … so what is your book about?

They are hard to write, but are critical elements that will go on your book cover.

The logline captures your main idea or question/your main character/the conflict they're going to face/the stakes if they lose. We're talking short and high-level concept.

This sentence utilizes puns or clever wording to intrigue the reader. It should make them want to read the book or learn more. It often teases the reader or poses a question to them. There is no formula. Just make your best effort for now.

Do not use names. Include the book title.

Some people claim that loglines should be less than 25 words. I don't think publishers and agents count the number of words in your logline; I think they want to understand the core story in one sentence.

How do you squish 50,000+ words into one line? Find the keywords.

Examples (Non-fiction):

- *In my Shoes* by Tamara Mellon tells the story of the Jimmy Choo founder's jaw-dropping life in the fashion business.
- *Fall Out: A Memoir of Friends Made and Friends Unmade* by Jane Street-Porter. Friends. Everyone needs them. Especially when relations between you and your family are less than perfect.
- *Find Your Extraordinary* by Jessica Herrin shows that you don't need to have it all to live an extraordinary life—you need to have what matters most to you.

WRITING TASK

Do your best and come up with at least five loglines with totally different angles and styles. Share them with your writing buddy or on the Facebook group to get some feedback and reactions.

TASK 42
The Elements of a Knockout Book Proposal

> 'Words are sacred. They deserve respect. If you get the right ones, in the right order, you can nudge the world a little.'
>
> **Tom Stoppard**

IF YOU WANT YOUR book to find a publisher or agent you need to present them with a business proposal that convinces them that your book is a great investment to make. This is where you stop being a writer and you start being an entrepreneur and self-advocate. Your book proposal is a business plan, plain and simple.

Remember what Tessa taught you about your Author Brand? Now it's time to pull it all together.

You are going to write your Book Proposal by working through the Cheat Sheet, leaving nothing out, to create what we call your PITCH DECK. You will be able to use all the elements of this hard-working document in different places once it is complete—our author blurb might sit on your website or the overview/blurb on the book sales page.

Do you very best and allow yourself a full week to get this document to the best version you can produce. This is the key to getting a publisher to notice you.

'itch deck cheat sheet

1. Book title + subtitle + genre

Titles are fantastically important and can sell a book. A non-fiction book title does not leave the reader guessing. It tells a reader exactly what the book is about. They are not vague, elusive—but they can be very clever. Choose something that will tell the publisher or reader what the book is about. You have been working on this throughout your book-writing process.

Like ...

- *The 7 Habits of Highly Effective People*
- *Rich Dad Poor Dad – What The Rich Teach Their Kids About*
- *Money That the Poor and Middle Class Do Not!*
- *The Tipping Point: How Little Things Can Make a Big Difference*

2. Book overview/blurb

Think of this as an executive summary or your back cover blurb. It needs to answer the question: What is your book about? It's short and snappy (around two to three paragraphs) and gives an overall idea of your book and its message. Make a clear, crafted and clever statement of what the book is about and why it is important.

3. About the author

You should already have tackled this in Part 3. Now you get to tweak it again. This is a third-person description of you and your brand. Think about how you would like to be introduced on a talk show. You are not really promoting yourself; you are promoting the book through you as an author. So take a deep breath and blow your own trumpet. It should be relevant to why you are writing the book and can be considered an authority. The agent or editor is looking for someone who stands out and can be marketed.

4. Book content

This is a longer version of the blurb and should include all spoilers or reveals. Aim for a maximum of two pages.

- ✓ What is this book about?
- ✓ What are the main points?
- ✓ Where does it take the reader?
- ✓ What are the highlights?
- ✓ What the key arguments/areas you cover?
- ✓ What topics are covered? What keywords can describe your book?

Keep your style good here, but make sure it also just covers the basics.

5. Similar titles

Which books are on the shelf next to yours? Be specific about the current competition for your reading audience, from the titles to the authors and their approach. What is your book going to compete with on the shelf? List big names in this genre. If you can't find any, you are not looking hard enough. Aim for around four to six in a list. This shows a publisher you have done your homework and understand the market.

6. Target market and reader

Be specific if you can, but also remember that publishers are looking for the most commercial books with the widest audience. If you show that there is a market for your book that is enough. Simply clearly state who will buy your books e.g. women age 35–50 with an interest in health. If you can link numbers to an audience it will support your case e.g.There are 55,000 homeowners who want to rent out and manage their own properties according to the latest Gallup Survey.

7. Visuals

This only applies to a book that includes photography (such as cookbooks or travel books) or illustrations. A publisher may want to see a sample of what the book is going to look like. It may be a good idea to spend some money if you are not doing the illustrations yourself. I highly recommend a few pages actually designed, or at least one illustration of what you have in mind. Don't go too far as the publisher may have their own layout artists, but if images are critical to your book, include some of them.

8. Marketing and promotions

The publisher is always considering the economics of your work. This is where you spell out how you will access your potential reader and help your publisher sell your books. You worked through Tessa's chapters, right?

We want fixed channels and numbers in this section. Think newsletters, blogs, websites, YouTube, LinkedIn, Facebook, and Instagram:

- ✓ Put numbers to each. For example, my newsletter 'Healthy Food Fast' has 5,000 subscribers.
- ✓ How else will you promote your book? Are you an accomplished public speaker? Do you do workshops? Can you run a course?
- ✓ List your last 12 talks. Make a note of the audience size.
- ✓ List your upcoming 12 months of speaking engagements. If you don't have any, set some up fast! Do not be tempted to fabricate here. Publishers will see right through it.

You can also offer to purchase a number of books from the publisher for back-of-the-room sales. This is not necessary, but they like it and it shows your commitment to sell the book.

9. A well-organized TOC

Keep your chapter titles explanatory. Your editor or agent should be able to look at the TOC and visualize the book. This of course depends on the type of book. Memoirs are different, as are humorous books. My preference is clarity over clever.

10. Attach your sample chapters

The sample chapters do not have to be long. But they need to be the best reflection of what the agent or publisher will be getting in the final book. It is worth putting in the time. Usually you will include your THREE best chapters. Typically you include your first chapter, and then choose two others that will best sell this book to potential publishers. They do not have to be chronological.

TASK 43

Write a Sizzling Author Query Letter

> 'We're all called.
> If you're here breathing, you have a contribution
> to make to our human community.'
> **Oprah Winfrey**

YOU HAVE WRITTEN YOUR LOGLINE and crafted your book proposal. You have written it again and again until it is darn near perfect. It sings. You have your entire pitch deck ready. Now what? How does this all come together?

You are going to send all these documents off to a publisher attached to a query letter, which is basically a well-crafted email.

It is the very first thing an agent or publisher is going to see. In the old days this used to be posted as a typed single sheet of paper. But now we tend to send email query letters or submit them online. Ideally, when the agent or publisher opens the email, they will see the main idea of your book in a few lines. This should closely resemble the back cover blurb, with a few tweaks.

What is essential is that you make them want to open the document attached to your email ... your knockout book proposal.

This high-level overview of your book must the answer the question: 'What is your book ABOUT?'

You will write one of these and then paste it into each letter you send to a publisher or agent. You will also copy and paste this into online submission platforms such as 'Submittable'.

Get your genre clear

State the title and genre in the body of the email. Phew, we got you covered here, right?

About your book

Go straight in and give them your best blurb. Grab the one from your book proposal. It should be around two to three short paragraphs. If you can't get it down ... work on it. The agent will decide if they want more of your book based on this basic summary, so do make sure you send your very best version.

About you

This is a short background that cues them into who you are. This is shorter than the full one in your proposal so get it down to around two to three sentences. Set yourself up as qualified to write this book. What is it that you do—are you a life coach, surgeon, proathlete, property broker? For a memoir, you need to highlight important things about yourself and your life.

Close it up

Phew! Almost done! Sign off. And that's all there is to it.

TASK 44
Sending Off to 'ublishers

> 'I wasn't going to give up until every single publisher turned me down,
> but I often feared that would happen.'
>
> **J.K. Rowling**

NOW THAT YOU HAVE DONE all the hard work, it's time to press play. If you want to get a publishing deal, this is where the rubber hits the road. You are going to be sending your book out to at least 20 traditional publishers or literary agents. The process is the same for both.

Remember, this is ultimately a sales game. Most writers will unfortunately not send their proposal to one publisher and magically get picked up by the first one. Yes, it can and does happen. If you are crystal clear on your genre, have a knockout proposal, know the current publishing climate, your book is highly contemporary/timeless/a great story or you have a big platform and author brand, then maybe the first publisher you approach will sign you up.

But please don't set yourself up for failure and lose hope if the first one sends you a rejection letter! The truth is that this is a long game, and along the journey you have to keep the momentum up, process any rejection letters, implement any feedback, get back to it, and keep going. Rinse and repeat. Rinse and repeat.

Author and motivational speaker Jack Canfield shares about how he approached 144 publishers with his little book *Chicken Soup for the Soul*. After 14 months he and co-author Mark Victor Hansen almost gave up.

Finally the 145th decided to take a chance on them—and has become a billion-dollar empire that is now a household name and has sold 500 million books. Imagine if they gave up after the first, 10th or 144th!

Step 1: Do your research

Remember we asked you to do some competitive research? We need to build on that now. Take a trip back to the bookshop. Find your genre, look on your own bookshelf, browse Amazon.com or Lulu.com to research publishing houses that fall on your dream publishing list. Make sure you also browse the internet to research all the publishing houses that might be a good fit.

Note down the relevant publisher's name. Choose most of your hit list as publishers based in your home country, and select at least four that are international.

Step 2: Build your hit list

Compile a list of at least 20 publishers and literary agents for your dream list. Do your research about who publishes books in your specific genre. Join online writing groups to network, connect and get ideas. Chat to any authors you know for leads and ideas. Follow relevant publishers on social media to stay up to date with their submission windows and publishing guidelines.

Step 3: Send to 20 in your first mail shot

Gone are the days of sending a printed and bound manuscript via the postal service. For the most part nowadays you will either be emailing the relevant commissioning editors, submission departments or submitting directly online through the publishing portal on the publisher's websites. Deep breath. And send.

A reminder of what you generally include to send off in your PITCH DECK:

- ✓ Your query letter – usually in the body of your email
- ✓ Your killer book proposal
- ✓ Your first three chapters attached to the email.

Remember three important things:

- ✓ Make sure they focus on YOUR GENRE
- ✓ Know their name (if relevant)
- ✓ Mention books similar to yours that they have published.

Some submission tips

- ✓ Be flexible. Some publishers will ask you to submit online and will allow only specific word counts for each section. Take your best versions and fit it into their formats
- ✓ Check their requirements first. Some don't want your first three chapters. Some want 10,000 words. Check if they want Word documents or PDFs
- ✓ Check if they have a naming protocol and follow it. Name your documents in a logical and consistent way. Usually, this is BOOK TITLE_synopsis and BOOK TITLE_Chapters
- ✓ Have all your documents properly formatted (read their requirements on font size and spacing) and add a footer on all documents that has this information: BOOK TITLE + AUTHOR NAME + DATE + PAGE NUMBER For example: *The Red Tent* by Sarah Agoran December 2018 page 1
- ✓ If you feel your book is not the best version yet, or your query letter needs work, then do this instead: Send your book to the publishers lower on your list. Save your hit list/

dream publisher submissions until you are clear it is your best version.

REMEMBER!

No matter how many books you have written, this is always the moment you have your heart in your throat. J.K. Rowling must have felt this again when she submitted her crime novel *The Cuckoo's Calling* under the pseudonym Robert Galbraith. Jo also sent her novel out to an estimated dozen publishers. Kate Mills, publishing director of Orion, was one of the publishers: 'When the book came in, I thought it was perfectly good,' she was quoted widely as saying. 'It was certainly well written—but it didn't stand out.'

TASK 45

What We Can Tell You About Getting Stuck and Moving On

> ‘The pathos, and the gift of life, is that we cannot know which will be our defining heartbreak, or our most victorious joy.’
>
> **Alexandra Fuller**

YOU HAVE MADE IT ALL the way! You wrote your book. Or did you?

If you have done it, we hope you feel proud of all the blood, sweat and tears you have poured into your project. All that is left now, is for you to sit tight, dig deep and keep sending off to publishers or agents. Just as in sales, it’s a numbers game, remember? Set weekly targets to stay motivated.

Check back every three months and send out again.

Or perhaps you are choosing the path of self-publishing? Then set new deadlines and learn the ropes fast. Don’t leave your book sitting around like so many other writers. Get the right support, mentoring and inspiration to see your dream come to fruition. Give yourself permission to hold your book in your hands.

Please keep us posted on your progress – your dream is important to us!

But what if you didn't finish? What if you are stuck? You would not be the first writer. Please reach out and connnect with us so we can get you over the finish line.

We can usually slot writers into one of five places where they might be stuck. Are you here? Sarah will guide you through the places in which you may find yourself. Any of them familiar?

You are stuck on just the idea of it

Yip, it is so easy to get stuck on the very IDEA of your book. So many possible stories swirling in your head. How should you start? Who should you include? Should you actually write about yourself? What research should you do? All writers have so many choices, but you are crippled with them.

Solution: Structure a solid writing plan. Go back to Part 1 and get a list of your book scenes together.

You are stuck on the first few chapters

And here is where many writers will get stuck. Some for years! This is one of my biggest slam-dunk-and-move-on areas I will rush you through. Any editor will tell you that you are never going to use those chapters as you first wrote them in your final draft, so stop agonizing and trying to perfect them. I am working with a writer on her eighth book and third draft of it.

'I am cutting out your first three chapters,' I told her. 'The rest of the book is fine but your story only really starts in Chapter 4.'

Gulp. All that work agonizing over those chapters and they are cut!

Solution: It will all change in your second draft so just do your best in the first round and move on. Did you read Sarah's Rules of Writing a first draft? Stick to them!

You are stuck at 20,000 words

You reach 20,000 words and now WHAT? You have told your whole story? But a book needs to be longer and you can see that now. What happened?

Solution: Plotting and structure need to happen! A book is long and that is why we require a certain number of plot points to take your story to the correct length. You might have to go back to the initial structure, chapter and scene list to dig deeper, expand your concept, bring in different aspects.

You are stuck on your first draft

So now you are a bit further down the line. Are you here now? You have pushed all the way to the end. It is a celebration. What do you do? Put it down and never touch it again. Hands up those who have done this? My hand is in the air as I have about four books sitting somewhere in my computer that I wrote and never did anything about.

Solution: Kate says time to pull finger and get ready to do some real work. All of you who have been working with us for a long time know that the first draft is just the START. After that, you will do your second draft and make it better.

Your first rejection letter

'Thank you so much for your submission but after careful consideration we regret to inform you book is not a good fit with our stable.' Crushing? Of course! So you sniff, delete that email, pretend it never happened and move on to things you are far better at. Right? No! This is the point at which you CANNOT STOP. Of course, not every publisher or agent will like your book. Nor will every reader.

Solution: Develop a thick skin. I like to call that a professional skin. We recommend sending to 20 publishers on your first email. Of this perhaps two will reply. So your first rejection will sting a bit, but the next few will hurt less.

Your job is to know your area of potential weakness, and find creative ways to move through them. That is IF you truly want your story to touch the lives of readers. And that's why you are still here, isn't it?

HEART EXERCISE

Remind yourself again of something we asked you right at the start. Why are you doing this?

Write a few sentences on each of these NOW—it might have changed from the first time, so don't look back at your answers.
Why this?
(Why this message? Why do people need to hear YOUR voice?)
Why me?
(Why not someone more experienced? Why do YOU need to tell this story?)
Why now?
(Why today? Why not tomorrow? Why not next year?)

And all that is left for us to say is follow your heart and do the work. Put in the time, blood, sweat and tears—and have some fun. Be sure to get the right support and see your project all the way to the shelves. We would love to see a picture of you with your final book and your beaming smile.

Kate and Sarah

What Our Writers Say …

I'm no writer but had a story I needed to tell. If you have a book 'inside' you and you have determination, then catch a ride with Sarah and Kate. Hold on tight—it won't be easy, and it does take time, but if you do it their way and do everything they say, you will get your first draft done. Their wealth of knowledge on the craft of writing, the industry, and process and the motivation around it all was priceless.

Costa Carastavrakis – *I Am Costa. From Meths To Marathons*

Four months of professional, caring, supporting and inspirational mentorship and guidance will ensure you get it done! When the opportunity came for both Kate and Sarah to mentor me for four months I jumped at the chance and now, with a plan, I was able to get started. I have never been more pleased with myself and my progress and the clarity that I have that will enable me to achieve this goal and my dream of having written a book. Without their guidance and the fact that we have to hold ourselves accountable, I am sure that I would have come to the end of this journey, called life, without leaving my legacy behind.

Gabi Lowe – *Get Me To 21*

This course was a big eye opener for me! It showed me that I can definitely write and publish a book, and that it's also not an exercise for the faint of heart! However, with the Mastermind structure it's much more accessible that just doing it in the dark … having the guidance, expertise and intense delivery context is definitely a potential game changer.

Brad Shorkend – *We Are Still Human: And Work Shouldn't Suck*

I loved the combination of Kate's inspiration and Sarah's taskmaster writing challenges.
Leigh Taylor – *The Mother Of All Myths*

Sarah and Kate's writing mentorship is the stick of dynamite you need to stop gazing at your own navel and instead gaze at a finish line that gets steadily closer. If you've been struggling to get your ideas out of your head and onto the page, this mentorship will prove invaluable.
Meg Chronis, Romance author

To turn your dreams into reality one needs to take action. This helps you to do just that. It gets the words moving from your head onto paper and your book becomes a reality.
Theresa Roberts – *Blind but Brilliant*

It was the hardest thing I've done and there were times I nearly chucked it in. I can proudly say I DO have that shi**y first draft!
Di Atherton – *Gate vs Di*

I never knew how to share my story, and then like a divine gift from the universe, came Kate and Sarah. From book structure and editing to publishing, branding and PR, I did it! And if I can, you can. What an incredible experience—let them show you how. It's a life-changing journey.
Jen Cole – *How to raise beautiful kids in an ugly world*

These two extraordinary women will take you on a journey you will never regret. I have challenged myself to test a dream. The tasks are very well thought through and keep one on track and it's wonderful to connect with other writers. It is a non-judgEmental course and process and therefore you can explore your writing without fear.
Caroline Menell

You are in for a ride of fun and learning, hard work, sleepless nights as well as the rousing and wondrous highs of meeting your own commitments in getting YOUR book done as you steadily come into your home run—your finish run—the draft of your book! Get your ticket now.

Hester Bergh Appoyer – *Being Nice Isn't Enough*

What an amazing and inspiring experience it has been. After sitting for years with bits and pieces of my second book done, I now have a completed first draft in my hands.

Jacqui Holmes – *Stained Glass for Beginners*

D-Day – Wow! What a journey. Yes I have a first draft! 89,000 words!

Carmen Tina Schneider

I absolutely loved the process with Kate Emmerson and Sarah Bullen. Not having been an author before, the experience gave me the grounding I needed to complete three chapters for a co-authored book and get started on my first book.

Bettina Pickering – *The Emotion Coach*

Kate cracks the whip and Sarah moulds your book into shape.

Sandra Buckingham

The people, the online community that was formed, the honesty and vulnerability and the opportunity we had to share stories, realizing that it wasn't just us, we weren't alone, sharing celebrations. What really worked was the commitment to the regular posts and you holding that firmly; the consistency was epic.

Wendy Ward – *Metamorphic Coaching and Presilience*

The two mentors synchronize and complement each other, not only in style, but in personalities as well. You are true professionals. Loved the feeling of how we were all connected despite the physical/geographical distances, how the group was handled, the instant, unwavering, and support. You played the role of an emotional rock, Kate. And you, Sarah, like a bullet, shooting right at the heart of the structural matter. This the only way to go, if you think you have a book!
Rena Rauch, Canada

ADDENDUM

List 1: Themes that bind your book

Abandonment	Good vs evil
Abuse	Gratitude
Accepting change	Grief
Adjusting to a new life	Growing up
Adventure	Guilt
Adoption	Heroes
Addiction	Heroism
Anger	History
Appearances	Home
Appreciation of nature	Honesty
Being gifted	Hope
Brotherhood	Humor
Bullies	Immigrants
Belonging	Initiation
Betrayal	Innocence
Bondage	Intergenerational relationships
Bravery	Invincibility
Caring for the environment	Jealousy
Censorship	Leadership
Challenges	Living

Change	Living in today's society
Coming of age	Loneliness
Commitment	Love
Communication	Loyalty
Community	Lying
Cooperation	Lust
Coping with loss	Making choices
Courage	Media
Crime	Morals and values
Honour	Obsession
Cultural diversity	Patriotism
Customs and traditions	Peace
Dealing with handicaps	Peer pressure
Death and dying	Poverty
Denial	Power
Depravity	Relationships
Determination	Revenge
Discrimination	Secrets
Diversity	Self-esteem
Dreams	Sense of community
Effects of war	Sense of self-separation and loss
Ethical dilemmas	Sex
Euthanasia	Shame
Evil	Social change
Family	Survival
Fear	Taking a stand
Forgiveness	Teamwork
Freedom	Trust

Friendship	Violence
Faith	War
Gender issues	

List 2: Amazon's categories of non-fiction

Arts & Photography

- Architecture
- Art
- Dance
- Fashion
- Graphic design
- Individual artists
- Music
- Performing arts
- Photography
- Theater

Biographies & Memoirs

- Arts & literature
- Ethnic & National
- Historical
- LGBT
- Leaders & Notable people
- Memoirs
- Professionals & Academics
- Reference & Collections
- Sports & Outdoor
- Travel
- True crime
- Women

Business & Investing

- Accounting
- Biography & History
- Business life

Economics
Education & Reference
Entrepreneurship & Small business
Finance
Green business
Industries
International
Investing
Job Hunting & Careers
Management & Leadership
Marketing & Sales
Organizational behavior
Personal finance
Real estate
Skills
Taxation
Technology
Women & Business

Children's Non-fiction

Animals
Arts & Music
Computers
History
People & Places
Philosophy
Politics & Government
Reference
Religions
Science
Nature & How it works
Sports & Activities

Children

Baby–2 years old

- Ages 3–5 years old
- Ages 6–8 years old
- Ages 9–12 years old
- Teen & Young adult
- K–12 Teachers

Computers & Technology

Cooking

- Baking
- Canning & Preserving
- Cooking by ingredient
- Culinary arts & Techniques
- Drinks & Beverages
- Gastronomy
- Meals
- Natural foods
- Outdoor cooking
- Professional cooking
- Quick & Easy
- Reference
- Regional & International
- Special appliances
- Special diet
- Special occasions
- Vegan & Vegetarian

Christian Books & Bibles

- Bibles
- Bible covers
- Bible study & Reference
- Biographies
- Catholicism
- Children's & Teens
- Christian denominations & Sects
- Christian living

Churches & Church leadership
Education
History
Literature & Fiction
Ministry & Evangelism
Protestantism
Romance
Theology
Worship & Devotion

Food & Wine Crafts

Crafts Hobbies & Home

Antiques & Collectibles
Crafts & Hobbies
Gardening & Horticulture
Home design
How-to & Home improvements

Humor & Entertainment

Coloring books for grown-ups
Humor
Movies
Performing arts
Pop culture
Puzzles & Games
Radio
Sheet music & Scores
Television
Trivia & Fun facts

Interior Design

Education & Reference

Engineering & Transportation

Health fitness & Dieting

- Addiction & Recovery
- Alternative medicine
- Beauty
- Grooming & Style
- Counseling & Psychology
- Death & Grief
- Diets & Weight loss
- Diseases & Physical ailments
- Exercise & Fitness
- Nutrition
- Personal health
- Reference
- Relationships
- Safety & First aid
- Sex
- Sports health & Safety
- Teen health

History

Law

Lesbian, Gay, Bisexual & Transgender Books

- Biographies & Memoirs
- Comics & Graphic novels
- LGBT studies
- Literature & Fiction
- Mystery & Thrillers
- Romance
- Science fiction & Fantasy
- Travel

Literary Criticism & Theory

Self-Help

- Creativity
- Eating disorders & Body image

Happiness
Inner child
Journal writing
Memory improvement
Motivational
Personal transformation
Self-Esteem
Spiritual
Stress management

Politics & Social Sciences

Anthropology
Archaeology
Philosophy
Politics & Government
Social Sciences
Sociology
Women's studies

Religion & Spirituality

Agnosticism

Atheism

Buddhism

Christian Books & Bibles

Hinduism

Islam

Judaism

Literature & Fiction

New Age & Spirituality

Occult & Paranormal

Other Eastern Religions & Sacred Texts

Other Religions, Practices & Sacred Texts

Religious Art

Religious Studies

Worship & Devotion

Reference

- Almanacs & Yearbooks
- Atlases & Maps
- Careers
- Catalogs & Directories
- Consumer guides
- Dictionaries & Thesauruses
- Encyclopedias & Subject guides
- English as a second language
- Etiquette
- Foreign language study & Reference
- Genealogy
- Quotations
- Survival & Emergency preparedness
- Test preparation
- Words, language & grammar
- Writing, research & Publishing guides

Science

Weddings

Sports

Teen & Young Adult

- Art, music & Photography
- Biographies
- Education & Reference
- Historical fiction
- Hobbies & Games
- Literature & Fiction
- Mysteries & Thrillers
- Personal health
- Religion & Spirituality

Romance
Science fiction & fantasy
Social issues
Sports & Outdoors

Travel

Food
Lodging & Transportation
Pictorial
Reference
Specialty travel
Travel writing
Africa
Asia
Australia & South Pacific
Canada
Caribbean
Central & South America
Europe
Middle East
Polar regions
United States

Parenting & Relationships

Adoption
Aging parents
Family activities
Family health
Family relationships
Fertility
Literature guides
Parenting
Reference
Special needs

Medical eBooks

Administration & Policy
Allied health professions
Alternative & Holistic
Basic science
Dentistry
Diseases
Education & Training
Internal medicine
Nursing
Pharmacology
Physician & Patient
Reference
Reproductive medicine & technology
Research
Specialties
Special topics
Veterinary medicine

List 3: Categories or subgenre of memoir

What if you are writing a memoir or biography?
Memoirs are as varied as their authors. Here are some of the most common types. Where will your memoir be placed? An escape, a journey, a transformation – these are the matters of memoir.

Celebrity

This one is obvious. Either YOU are famous or you are the family/sibling/child of a famous person. Any level of fame is appropriate and there are readers for every type of famous person, from church leaders, serial killers, politicians, community leaders and literary figures to mega stars. Readers are interested in an insider view of your life with this person.

For example:

- *Believe Me: A Memoir of Love, Death, and Jazz Chickens* by Eddie Izzard
- *Becoming* by Michelle Obama
- *Extreme!* by Sharon Osbourne
- *Sisters First, Stories from our Wild and Wonderful Life* by Jenna Bush Hager and Barbara Pierce Bush

If you are NOT a celebrity (or writing about one) your book will fall into one of the following categories:

1. Extraordinary Stories

This is a very general category but in these books you meet pretty regular people who have done amazing and recognized things from building a clinic in Afghanistan (*Three Cups of Tea* by Greg Mortenson and David Oliver Relin) to running the Great Wall of China (*Running Barefoot* by Amy Harmon). This is if you have DONE something and have a story to share.

Most of these fall into a story structure I call 'I did it/It happened to me' and tell the stories about how the author overcame odds or found solutions. They can be about anything ... moving to a remote village, teaching English in Cambodia, dreadful families, health, abuse, marrying a mobster, weight loss, fitness, disease, accidents, disasters, divorces, drinking, drugs, murder, prison … the list goes on. They often contain a personal solution and a personal message.

For example:

- *I am Malala* by Malala Yousafzai
- *Running Barefoot* by Amy Harmon
- *Three Cups of Tea* by Greg Mortenson

2. Health (general)

This is a general category (shelf) and see below if you can segment it. It can be a frank discussion of how you dealt with a health problem, big or small. It can be your own, a child's, family member or friend. Examples are: Parkinson's disease, diabetes, obesity, autism, cancer, Myalgic Encephalomyelitis (ME). A book like this needs to give some sort of hope and practical advice and solutions—even if not an answer.

For example:

- *Tell Me Everything You Don't Remember: The Stroke That Changed My Life* by Christine Hyong-Oak Lee

- *Get Me to 21, The Jenna Lowe Story* by Gabi Lowe
- *Sick: A Memoir* by Porochrista Khakpour

3. Medical Survival

These memoirs are often about medical emergencies, terrible accidents, a fight back to life, or a blow-by-blow account of the accident and recovery (or not). A life-and-death struggle. They often have a shorter time frame than a long health journey.

For example:

- *When Breath Becomes Air* by Paul Kalanithi
- *The Diving Bell and the Butterfly* by Jean-Dominique Bauby
- *Brain on Fire: My Month of Madness* by Susannah Cahalan

4. Cult/Religious Sect Insider

Typically written by someone who was part of a cult, under the influence of a guru, or who has an insider view on a religious sect or religion such as Scientology, Seventh Day Adventists, Islam, Isis, yoga, or who is even perhaps a guru's lover …

For example:

- *Escape* by Carolyn Jessop
- *Beyond Belief: My Secret Life Inside Scientology and My Harrowing Escape* by Jenna Miscavige Hill
- *In the Days of Rain: A Daughter, A Father, A Cult* by Rebecca Stott

5. Inspirational/Spiritual

This is a very broad category. It is about sin, searching and redemption played out as a personal quest. These can be warm and funny or deep and meaningful, or any flavor in between. It can include any religion although each religion will fall into its own category (and often shelf in a bookstore)

For example:

- *Eat, Pray, Love* by Elizabeth Gilbert.
- *Girl Meets God* by Lauren F Winner
- *The Faith Club: A Muslim, a Christian, A Jew: Three Women Search for Understanding* by Suzanne Oliver

6. Spiritual – Near-death experience (NDE)

These very specific stories need to include a NDE and include the descriptions of coming back.

For example:

- *Dying to be Me, My Journey From Cancer, to Near Death, to True Healing* by Anita Moorjani.
- *Proof of Heaven, A Neurosurgeon's Journey into the Afterlife* by Eben Alexander

7. Spiritual/Inspirational (Expert)

You need to be a practitioner of some sort to write this. Traditionally, this would be more of a non-fiction book, but the lines can cross. You can be a life coach, transformation coach, religious leader, breath work guide, shaman, and so on. The difference here is important; you are sharing your story, but you are also sharing processes, techniques, recommendations or solutions to the 'layman'.

For example:

- *The Seven Spiritual Laws of Success* by Deepak Chopra
- *The Power of Now* by Eckhart Tolle
- *Finding your own North Star* by Martha Beck
- *You Can Heal your Life* by Louise Hay

8. Business

This is more cut and dried and a very popular category. It includes any memoir that details your work life, success, failures, rise, fall, triumphs or success—from big business, corporate, entrepreneurs, hairdressers, and make-up artists. Please note if you are a recognized name or a celebrity, this will fall under 'Celebrity/Business'.

For example (celebrity):

- *Screw It, Let's Do It* by Richard Branson
- *Lean In: Women, Work and the Will to Lead by* Sheryl Sandberg

For example (not celebrity):

- *Good to Great* by Jim Collins.
- *Slacker MBA: A Business Memoir* by Michael Pollard
- *How to Fail in Sales* by Derek Wykeham
- *Setting the Table: The Transforming Power of Hospitality in Business* by Danny Meyer

9. Food

This is a new and very popular genre. It can take almost any form but it is an ode to your love of food, relationship with food, or food solutions for others. This is not a cookbook genre but a memoir wrapped around food.

For example:

- *Trail of Crumbs. Hunger, Love and the Search for Home* by Kim Sunee
- *My Life in France* by Julia Child
- *Kitchen Confidential* by Anthony Bourdain
- *Blood, Bones and Butter: The Inadvertent Education of a Reluctant Chef* by Gabrielle Hamilton

- *I Loved, I Lost, I Made Spaghetti: A Memoir of Good Food and Bad Boyfriends* by Guilia Melucci

10. Family and parenting

These are memoirs, often amusing, about family relationships and life with kids. They will often sit on the parenting shelf rather than the general memoir shelf. They can be solution-driven or simply confessions of parenting woes, mishaps or realities. Bad Mom, Fussy Pot Mom, Strict Mom, Drunk Dad, Bossy Dad …

For example:

- *Battle Hymn of the Tiger Mother* by Amy Chua
- *Stuck in the Middle with You: A memoir of parenting three genders* by Jennifer Finney Boylan
- *Confessions of a Paris Potty Trainer: A humorous parenting memoir* by Vicki Lesage

11. Travel

Your journey. Any journey. It can be to other countries, on the road, a hike, a pilgrimage. This is a specific genre and readers know it and like it. It can be amusing, dramatic, factual, descriptive, laced with food, wine, sex, dating or culture.

For example:

- *Notes from a Big Country* by Bill Bryson
- *Down the Nile Alone in a Fisherman's Skiff* by Rosemary Mahoney
- *Africa Trek* by Sonia and Alexandre Poussin
- *Wild* by Cheryl Strayed

12. I survived

Surviving a terrible boss, loss, war, starvation, disease, poverty, a beating, decades of abuse, drug abuse, illness or mania. These are stories of courage where the writer overcame harrowing circumstances and beat incredible odds. They can sit on the 'inspirational' shelf or on the 'biography general' shelf.

For example:

- *I Know Why the Caged Bird Sings* by Maya Angelou
- *I Have Life* by Alison Botha
- *A Boy Called It* by David Pelzer
- *Behind Closed Doors: A Daughter's Story* by Daniella DeChristopher
- *Manic: A Memoir* by Terri Cheney

13. Zeitgeist

This is a genre I am lumping together. It is a memoir that evokes a certain time gone by and captures readers interested in this time. There is a large demand for these memoirs. They can fall into specific time periods or places—like the Holocaust, Rhodesia, Vietnam, Baby Boomers. The story does not have to be extraordinary, but more to really make come to life a time, era or setting.

For example:

- *Don't Let's go to the Dogs Tonight* by Alexandra Fuller
- *Running with Scissors* by Augusten Burroughs

14. Expert non-fiction

You need to be an expert or professional practitioner of some sort to write this. You could be a sales expert, business or life coach, yoga teacher, car mechanic, businessman, or shaman. The difference here with a non-expert is important; you are sharing your story but you are also sharing processes, techniques, recommendations or solutions to the 'layman'. This can be a workbook or straight non-fiction,

For example:

- *The Dukan Diet* by Dr Pierre Dukan
- *How to Win Friends and Influence People* by Dale Carnegie
- *You Can Heal Your Life* by Louise Hay

15. Expert non-fiction (Business-to-business / Expert-to-professional)

This is when an expert in a particular field is writing for other professionals in the field. This may cover how to improve your professional expertise and develop your continued professional development (CPD).

For example:

- *Hacking Marketing: Agile Practices to Make Marketing Smarter, Faster, and More Innovative* by Scott Brinker
- *Content Inc.: How Entrepreneurs Use Content to Build Massive Audiences and Create Radically Successful Businesses* by Joe Pullizi

List 4: 'ersonality Traits

Accessible	Dynamic	Intuitive	Responsible
Active	Earnest	Inventive	Responsive
Adaptable	Ebullient	Kind	Romantic
Admirable	Educated	Knowledgeable	Scholarly
Adventurous	Efficient	Leader	Scrupulous
Affectionate	Elegant	Logical	Secure
Agreeable	Eloquent	Lovable	Self-confident
Ambitious	Emotional	Loving	Self-disciplined
Amiable	Empathetic	Loyal	Selfless
Amusing	Energetic	Magnanimous	Sensible
Appreciative	Enthusiastic	Many-sided	Sensitive
Articulate	Exciting	Meticulous	Sentimental
Aspiring	Extraordinary	Mature	Serious
Balanced	Exuberant	Methodical	Sexy
Benevolent	Fair	Moderate	Sharing
Brave	Faithful	Modest	Shrewd
Bright	Farsighted	Multi-leveled	Simple
Brilliant	Fearless	Neat	Sincere
Broad-minded	Firm	Objective	Skilful
Calm	Flexible	Observant	Sociable
Capable	Focused	Open	Sophisticated
Captivating	Forgiving	Optimistic	Spontaneous
Caring	Forthright	Orderly	Steadfast
Challenging	Frank	Organized	Steady

Charismatic	Freethinking	Original	Stoic
Charming	Friendly	Passionate	Straightforward
Cheerful	Fun-loving	Patient	Strong
Clear-headed	Funny	Patriotic	Studious
Clever	Generous	Peaceful	Suave
Colorful	Gentle	Perceptive	Subtle
Communicative	Genuine	Perfectionist	Sweet
Compassionate	Good-natured	Persistent	Sympathetic
Confident	Gracious	Personable	Systematic
Conscientious	Hardworking	Persuasive	Tasteful
Considerate	Healthy	Philosophical	Thorough
Contemplative	Hearty	Pioneering	Thoughtful
Cooperative	Helpful	Playful	Tidy
Courageous	Heroic	Powerful	Tolerant
Courteous	High-minded	Practical	Tough
Creative	Honest	Precise	Tractable
Cultured	Honourable	Principled	Trusting
Curious	Humble	Pro-active	Understanding
Daring	Humorous	Profound	Upright
Decent	Idealistic	Protective	Urbane
Decisive	Imaginative	Prudent	Venturesome
Dedicated	Impartial	Purposeful	Versatile
Deep	Impressive	Punctual	Vivacious
Determined	Incisive	Quick-witted	Warm
Dignified	Incorruptible	Rational	Well-read
Diligent	Independent	Realistic	Well-rounded
Diplomatic	Individualistic	Reflective	Well-traveled
Directed	Innovative	Relaxed	Willing

Disciplined	Inoffensive	Reliable	Wise
Discreet	Insightful	Reserved	Witty
Dramatic	Intellectual	Resourceful	
Dutiful	Intelligent	Respectful	

List 5: Values 'ersonal

Ability	Depth	Hospitality	Qualification
Abundance	Desire	Humility	Quality
Acceptance	Determination	Humor	Realistic
Accomplishment	Development	Imagination	Reason
Accountability	Differentiation	Impact	Recognition
Accuracy	Dignity	Impartiality	Refinement
Achievement	Diligence	Impeccability	Reflection
Acknowledgement	Diplomacy	Improvement	Relationships
Adaptability	Direction	Independence	Reliability
Adequacy	Directness	Individuality	Resilience
Adventure	Discipline	Ingenuity	Resolution
Affective	Discovery	Innovation	Resourcefulness
Affluence	Discretion	Inquisitiveness	Respect
Alertness	Diversity	Insightfulness	Responsibility
Ambition	Dreaming	Inspiration	Responsiveness
Amusement	Drive	Instinctiveness	Results
Appreciation	Duty	Integrity	Risk taking
Approachability	Effectiveness	Intelligence	Sacrifice
Artfulness	Efficiency	Intensity	Satisfaction
Assertiveness	Elegance	Intuition	Security
Assurance	Empathy	Intuitiveness	Self-awareness
Attention to detail	Empowering	Invention	Self-motivation
Attentiveness	Encourage	Inventiveness	Self-responsibility
Authenticity	Encouragement	Investment	Self-control

Availability	Endurance	Joy	Self-realization
Awareness	Energy	Justice	Selflessness
Balance	Enjoyment	Kindness	Service
Boldness	Enthusiasm	Knowledge	Significance
Bravery	Entrepreneurship	Knowledge	Silliness
Brilliance	Environment	Leadership	Simplicity
Buoyancy	Equality	Learning	Sincerity
Calmness	Excellence	Level-headed	Skilfulness
Camaraderie	Excitement	Liberation	Smartness
Candor	Experience	Liveliness	Sophistication
Capability	Expertise	Logic	Spontaneity
Certainty	Exploration	Longevity	Stability
Challenge	Expressiveness	Loyalty	Status
Character	Exuberance	Maturity	Stewardship
Clarity	Facilitating	Maximum utilization	Stillness
Cleverness	Fairness	Meaning	Strength
Closeness	Faithfulness	Meticulousness	Structure
Cognizance	Fame	Mindfulness	Substantiality
Collaboration	Family	Modesty	Success
Comfort	Fascination	Motivation	Sufficiency
Commitment	Fearless	Obedience	Support
Common sense	Firmness	Open-mindedness	Surprise
Communication	Flexibility	Openness	Sustainability
Community	Flow	Optimism	Sympathy
Compassion	Fluency	Order	Synergy
Competence	Fluidity	Originality	Tactfulness

Competition	Focus	Partnership	Talent
Composure	Foresight	Passion	Teamwork
Concentration	Fortitude	Peacefulness	Timeliness
Confidence	Frankness	Perceptiveness	Tolerance
Confidentiality	Freedom	Perfection	Transparency
Conformity	Friendliness	Performance	Trustworthiness
Congruency	Friendship	Perseverance	Truth
Connection	Frugality	Persistence	Understanding
Consciousness	Fun	Personal growth	Uniqueness
Consideration	Generosity	Playfulness	Unity
Consistency	Gentility	Positivity	Unselfishness
Continuity	Genuineness	Potency	Variety
Contribution	Giving	Potential	Victory
Control	Goal-oriented	Power	Vigor
Conviction	Goodwill	Practicality	Virtue
Cooperation	Grace	Precision	Vision
Coordination	Gratefulness	Preparedness	Vitality
Correct	Gratitude	Presence	Vivacity
Courage	Greatness	Preservation	Warmth
Courtesy	Growth	Pride	Watchfulness
Creativity	Guidance	Privacy	Wealth
Credibility	Happiness	Proactivity	Welcoming
Curiosity	Hard work	Productivity	Wholesomeness
Daring	Harmony	Professionalism	Willfulness
Decisiveness	Health	Proficiency	Willingness
Dedication	Honesty	Profitability	Winning
Deepness	Honour	Progress	Wisdom
Dependability	Hopefulness	Prosperity	Work/Life balance

Tips for Acing 'Bum Time' and Block Writing Sessions

1. Clock in and out

Be specific, and mindful when you start and when you finish. A focused strategy is better than just wafting into your block time writing. Make it matter!

Clock in with yourself, connect with your buddy if you have one, check in with the Facebook group or team up with another writer in your city.

2. Set a specific target

Setting aside the hours is one thing; creating a SPECIFIC target for each block time session is far more compelling. This applies to every writing session and, for bum time, it becomes even more critical.

Be bold. Pick a significant number and just go for it.

As a guideline, aim for a MINIMUM of 2,000 words per sitting.

Your specific target might be different:

- ✓ Write 4,000 words.
- ✓ Complete my scene list and write 1,500 words.
- ✓ Write three scenes today.
- ✓ Create a cover idea and write 1,000 words.

You will probably type faster than ever before as you near your day's deadline. Don't stress too much about fixing as you write. You can go back and do a basic spell/grammar check at the end of your sitting.

3. Think boy scouts/girl guides – be prepared

If you are going to a coffee shop, give your technology some forethought. Take adaptors, chargers, and extension cords – everything you need to stay connected.

Take a cushion, even if your destination has cushions. We often find coffee-shop cushions are too thin to sit on for hours at a stretch. Take something to keep warm. When you sit for an extended period of time, your body temperature CAN drop. We find one of the most important tech gadgets is a pair of good-quality earphones – perhaps you don't like the music, or a noisy neighbor starts distracting you.

4. Stay energized

Move often to get up and stretch your body and bones. Keep your breath deep and flowing, and your blood circulating. Sitting for too long can have the opposite effect on your writing and your energy might start slumping, as does your posture. Also think about what you are putting into your body and snack well – keep sugar to a minimum, protein high and lots of water for enhanced executive functioning.

Happy body and brain = WORDS FLOW!

5. Manage your distractions

Do whatever you need to do to not get distracted. Put your phone on airplane mode (or at least silent), switch off your email and take care of all other potential distractions. If you know it takes you 15 minutes to settle, build that into your bum time strategy

Above all – revel in the time you have created for this project!

Printed by Amazon Italia Logistica S.r.l.
Torrazza Piemonte (TO), Italy

60094672R00141